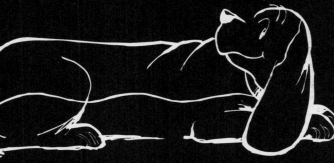

Fred Basset

CELEBRATING 50 YEARS

FRED BASSET: CELEBRATING 50 YEARS

Drawings by Alex Graham and Michael Martin

Summersdale Publishers Ltd
46 West Street
Chichester
West Sussex
PO19 1RP
UK

www.summersdale.com

Printed and bound in China

ISBN: 978-1-84953-409-3

Substantial discounts on bulk quantities of Summersdale books are available to corporations, professional associations and other organisations. For details contact Nicky Douglas by telephone: +44 (0) 1243 756902, fax: +44 (0) 1243 786300 or email: nicky@summersdale.com.

Fred Basset

1963
=to=
2013

CELEBRATING **50** YEARS

FOREWORD

My father, Alex Graham, would have been amazed to see Fred turn 50. When Associated Newspapers first commissioned the strip it was for an initial period of just six months, but the years have flown by to this landmark. The statistics are rather impressive: multiplying 364 days a year by 50 – leaving aside Christmas Day and leap years – comes to over 18,000 strips. This figure represents the number of original pieces of artwork. Alistair (my husband) and I try our best not to repeat an idea, but with this weight of material it is almost impossible.

I am frequently asked 'How do you think up the ideas?' and 'How does it work with Michael Martin, your artist, living in South West France?' Well, it works like this: I carry a notebook, as does Alistair, and we jot down anything we observe or hear which we think might work as an idea. Catchphrases or expressions used on the radio or television, especially cookery programmes, can be a good source (apologies for that!).

The next stage is to expand the idea into a storyline; this can be the most challenging part. Some ideas are quite amenable, whilst others can prove stubborn and unworkable. Alistair and I often work at these storylines over 'a pie and a pint' or, in my case, a glass of white wine and something more delicate!

Then it's down to Michael, who draws up roughs based on the storylines and sends them over by email or fax. These roughs will contain Michael's own contributions, not just to the original concept but also new twists for the storyline. It is at this stage that personal contact is vital so that discussions can take place and the strip can be finalised. Many of our meetings take place in South West France, close to the Pyrenees. Although hitherto unknown in France, Fred has won many friends in the area and takes part in the annual Festival of Cartoons in St Gaudens. It was a proud moment when the local newspaper *La Dépêche* declared that *'Fred Basset est Commingeois'* ('Fred Basset is one of us').

Michael then refines the artwork and adds the lettering ready for publication. Even the finished strip needs to be edited for any error in grammar, spelling or continuity.

Whilst adhering to the original concept, Fred has developed both in design and with the introduction of new characters. For example, he has changed shape to a fuller figure (don't we all!). Jock and Yorky have been joined by Taffy, a little Welsh terrier. Lucy and Jemma, our two cocker spaniels, also make appearances. On the human side, Fred's master and mistress have befriended a Frenchman named Claude, whilst Amanda has Mia for a playmate. Sam is a modern teenager, while the Tucker Twins are still up to their tricks, and the Barrington-Smyths, the Vicar and the long-suffering butcher put in regular appearances.

The selection in this book covers each of Fred's 50 years and reflects many of the themes, characters and escapades of our hero. I hope you enjoy it.

Happy Birthday, Fred!

Arran Graham

ACKNOWLEDGEMENTS

I am indebted to everyone at Summersdale for making this book possible. A special thank you goes to Chris Turton who went through every Fred Basset annual and advised on the choice. One of his colleagues described him as 'Fredded out', but he was still smiling when I saw him.

1963

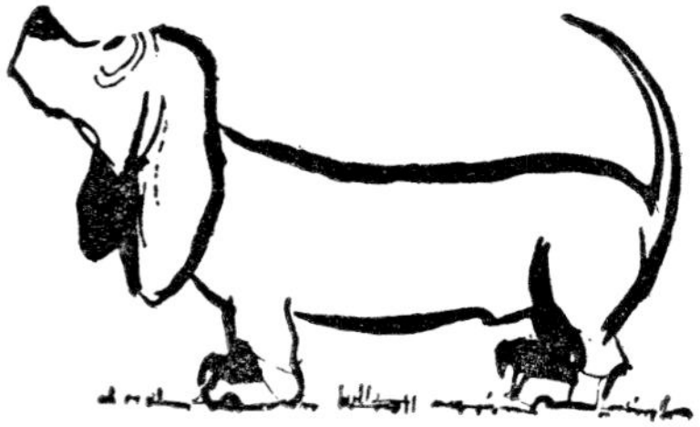

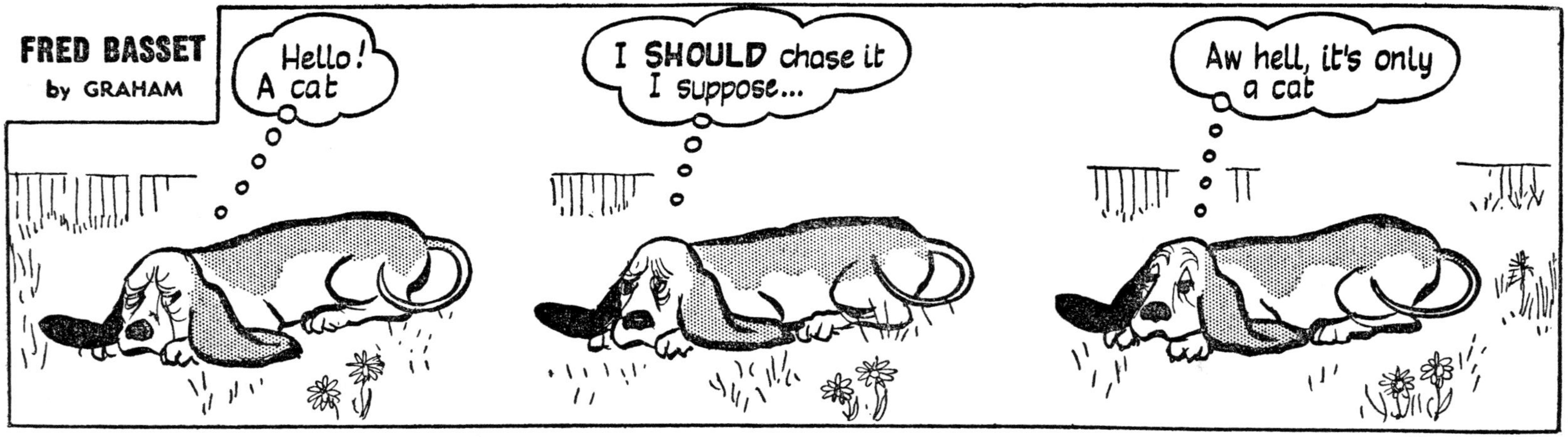
FRED BASSET
by GRAHAM
Hello! A cat
I SHOULD chase it I suppose...
Aw hell, it's only a cat

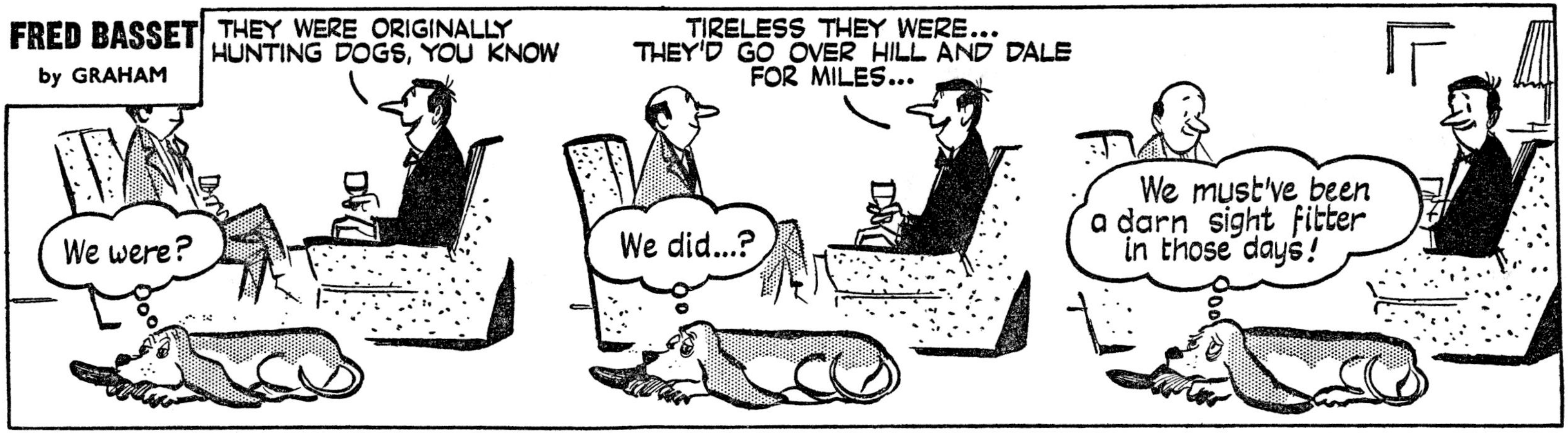
FRED BASSET
by GRAHAM
THEY WERE ORIGINALLY HUNTING DOGS, YOU KNOW
We were?
TIRELESS THEY WERE... THEY'D GO OVER HILL AND DALE FOR MILES...
We did...?
We must've been a darn sight fitter in those days!

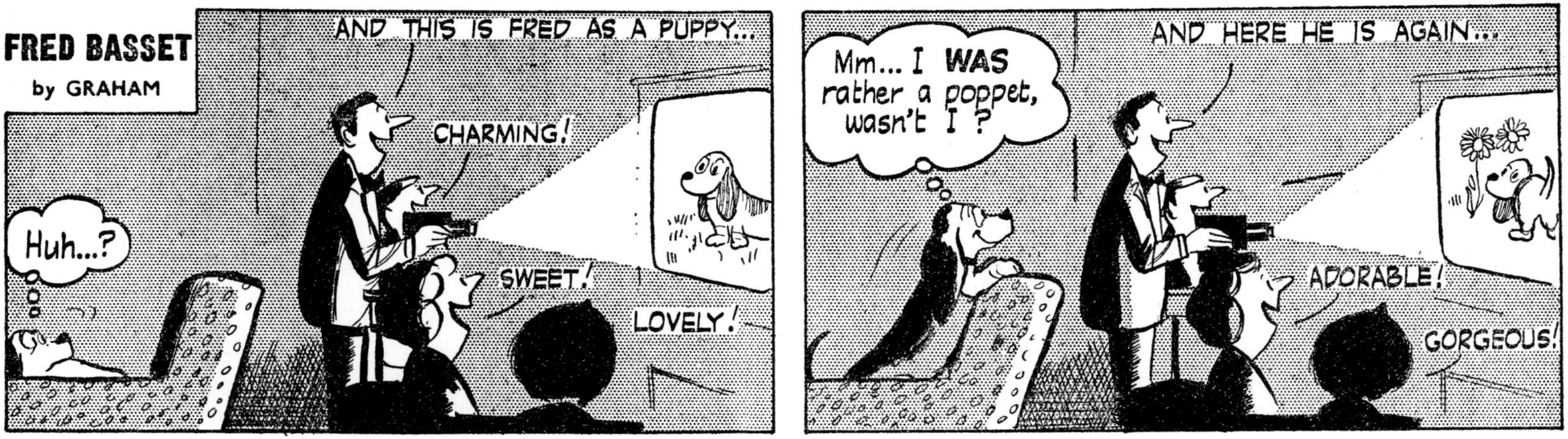
FRED BASSET
by GRAHAM
AND THIS IS FRED AS A PUPPY...
CHARMING!
Huh...?
SWEET!
LOVELY!
AND HERE HE IS AGAIN...
Mm... I **WAS** rather a poppet, wasn't I ?
ADORABLE!
GORGEOUS!

1964

FRED BASSET
by GRAHAM
THE BEATLES
The Beatles, eh?
THE BEATLES
Now that name's got a familiar ring... Beatles...Beatles...
It'll come to me in a minute... I'm sure there was something in the papers about them just the other day

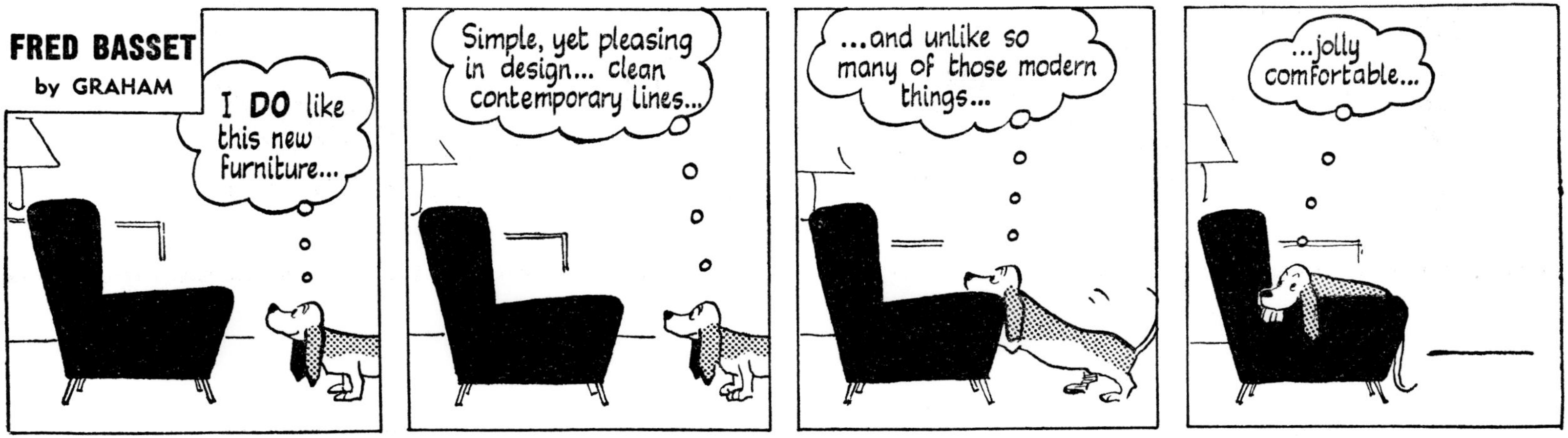
FRED BASSET
by GRAHAM
I DO like this new furniture...
Simple, yet pleasing in design... clean contemporary lines...
...and unlike so many of those modern things...
...jolly comfortable...

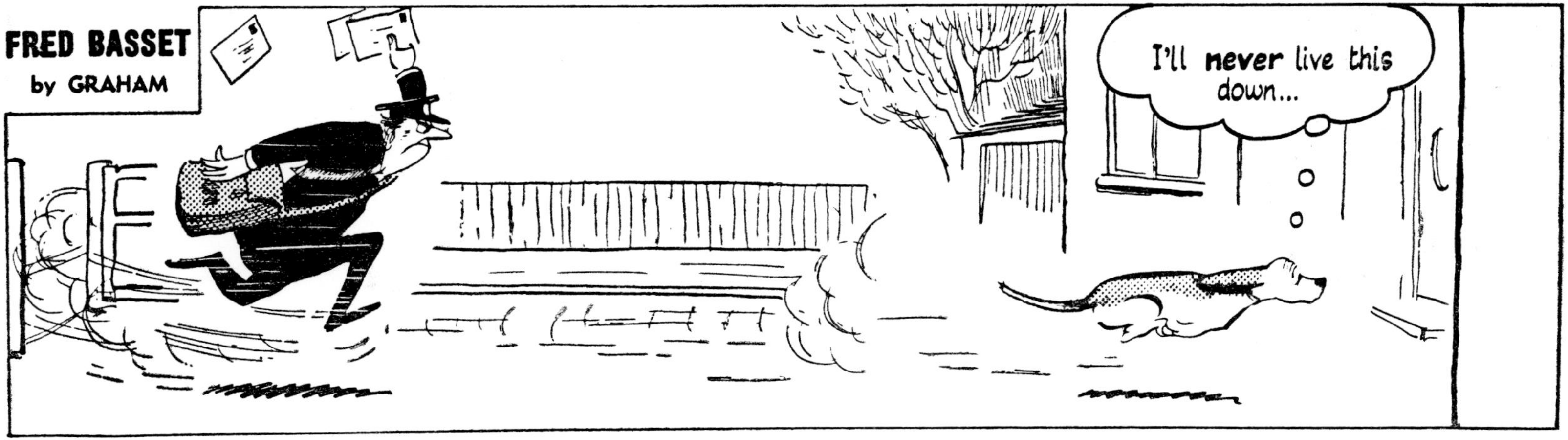
FRED BASSET
by GRAHAM
I'll never live this down...

1965

FRED BASSET
by GRAHAM
Courage, chaps!...Stand firm!... Let no single one of us flinch!... One for all, and all for one!
This neighbourhood's been dominated for far too long by Mrs. Lovibond's cat

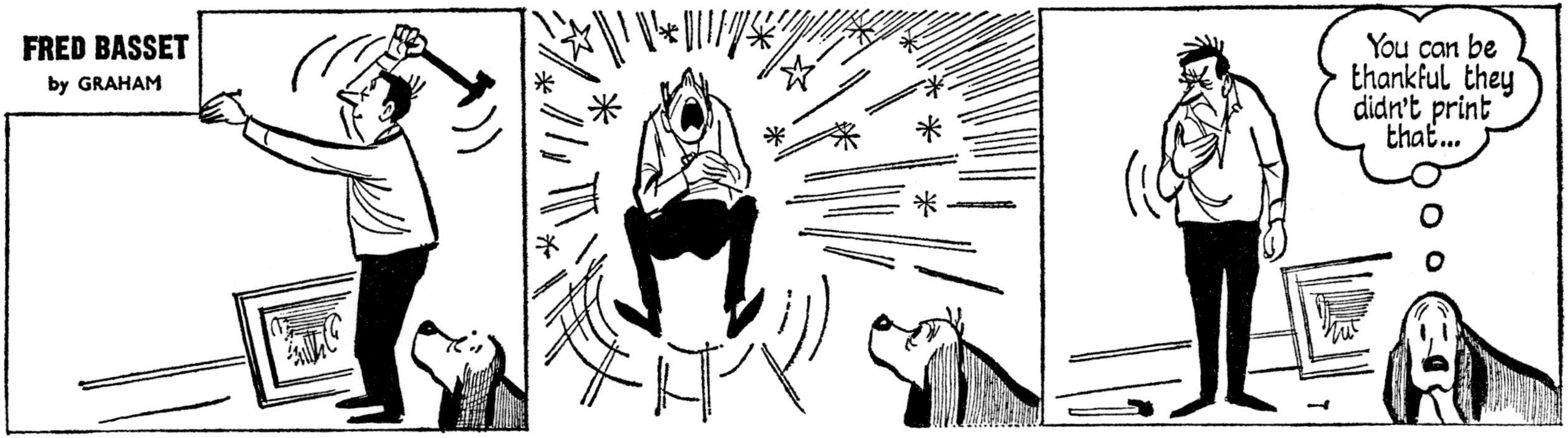
FRED BASSET
by GRAHAM
You can be thankful they didn't print that...

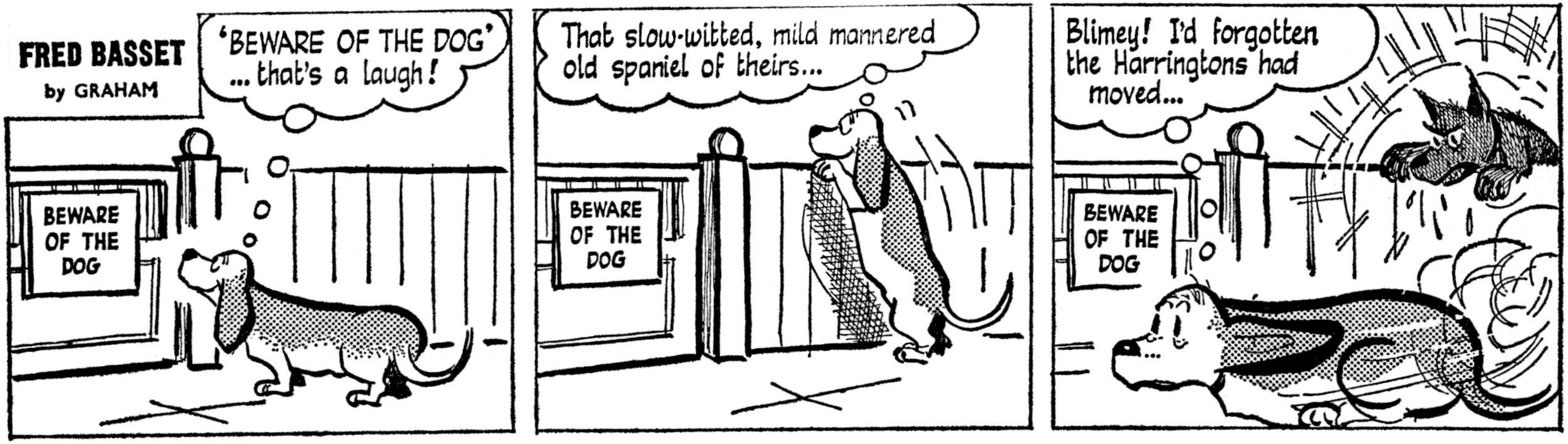
FRED BASSET
by GRAHAM
'BEWARE OF THE DOG' ... that's a laugh!
BEWARE OF THE DOG
That slow-witted, mild mannered old spaniel of theirs...
BEWARE OF THE DOG
Blimey! I'd forgotten the Harringtons had moved...
BEWARE OF THE DOG

1966

FRED BASSET by GRAHAM

Here's what happened!... In chasing the cat I unseated the little boy from his bicycle, which careered on and knocked the window-cleaner off his ladder, which slid down and broke the butcher's window, showering the policeman with glass... All my fault, I suppose!

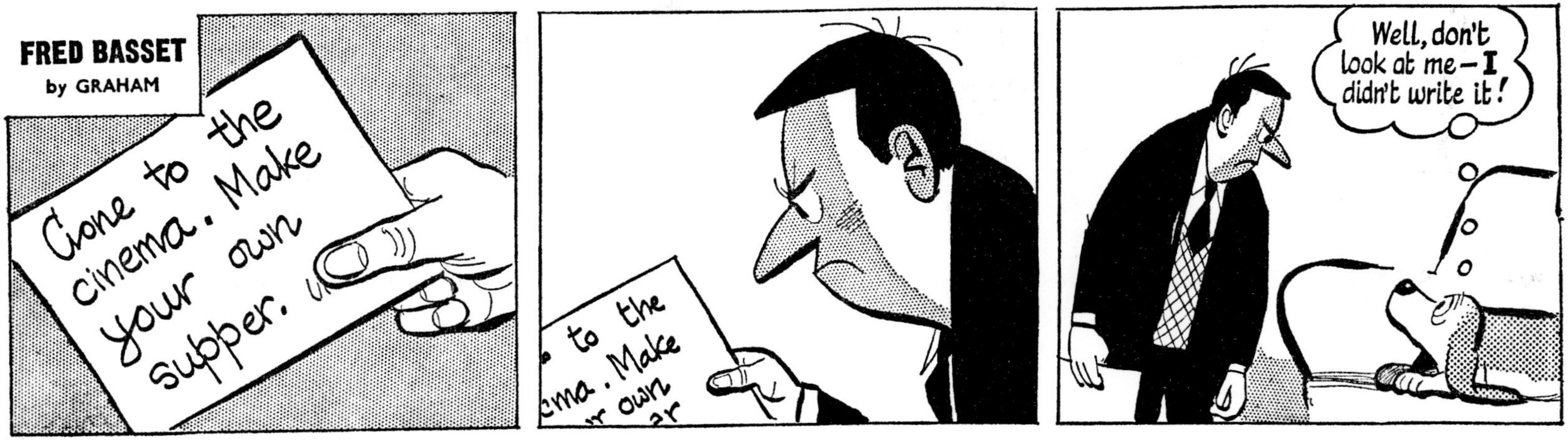
FRED BASSET
by GRAHAM
Gone to the cinema. Make your own supper.
to the cma. Make r own
Well, don't look at me—I didn't write it!

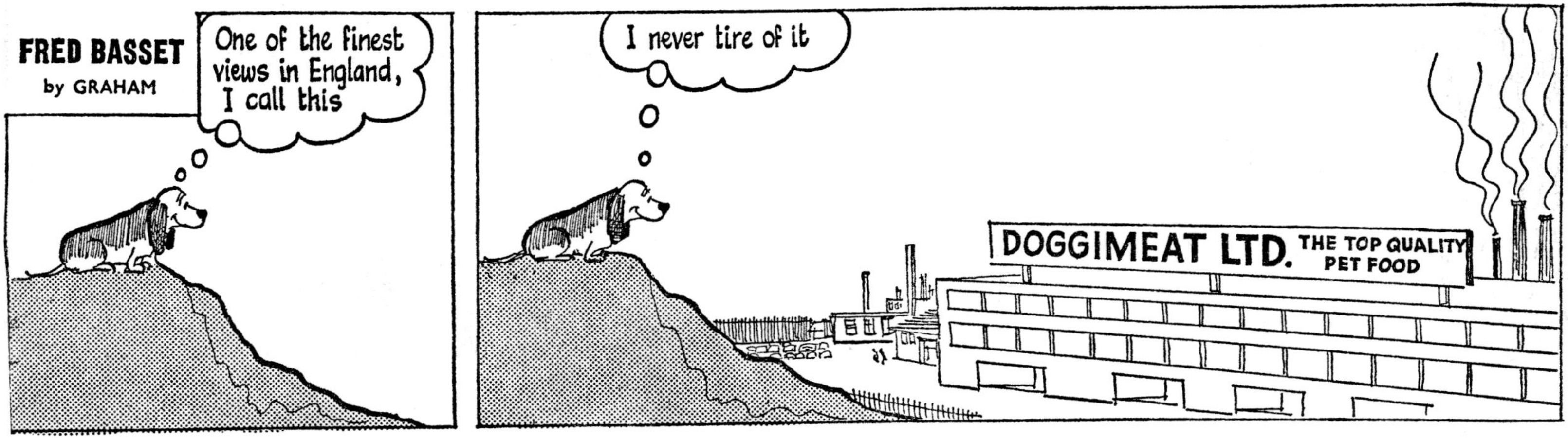
FRED BASSET
by GRAHAM
One of the finest views in England, I call this
I never tire of it
DOGGIMEAT LTD. THE TOP QUALITY PET FOOD

1967

FRED BASSET
by GRAHAM
Ooh la-la — La belle Fifi...
Très chic ... Quelle élégance... Enchanté
Believe me, there aren't many bi-lingual bassets around!

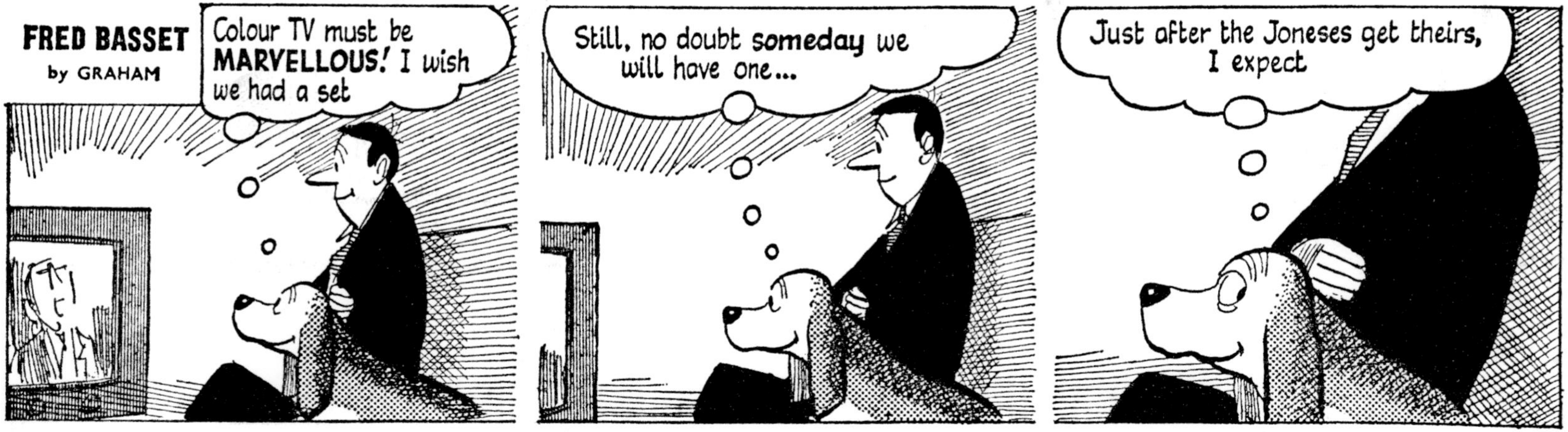
FRED BASSET
by GRAHAM
Colour TV must be MARVELLOUS! I wish we had a set
Still, no doubt someday we will have one...
Just after the Joneses get theirs, I expect

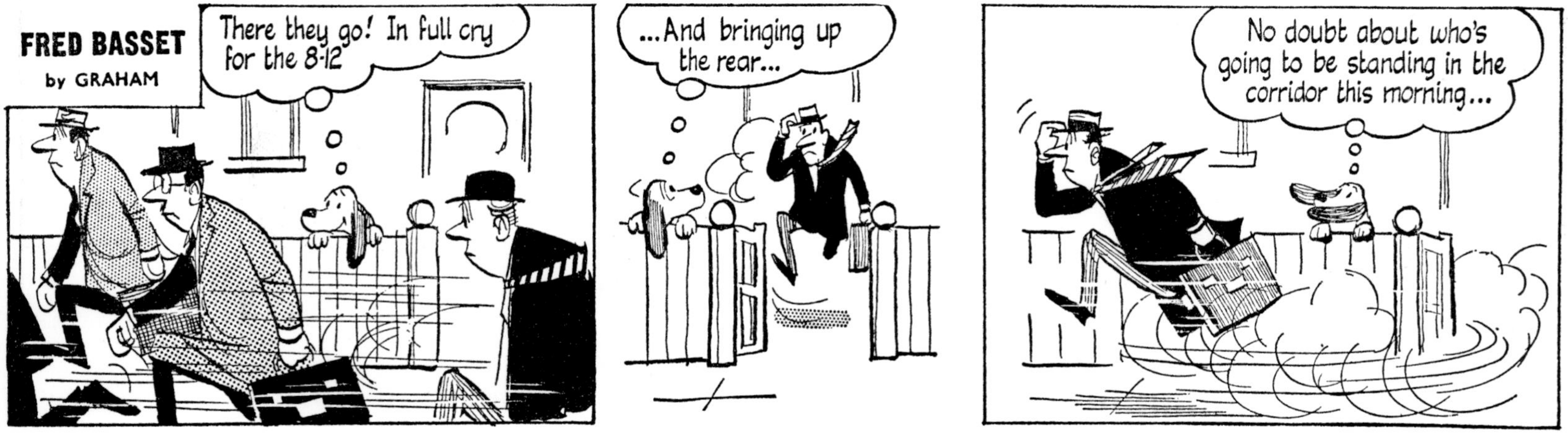
FRED BASSET
by GRAHAM
There they go! In full cry for the 8·12
...And bringing up the rear...
No doubt about who's going to be standing in the corridor this morning...

1968

FRED BASSET
by GRAHAM
ARE YOU SITTING COMFORTABLY ?
...THEN I'LL BEGIN
Good !
Just made it !

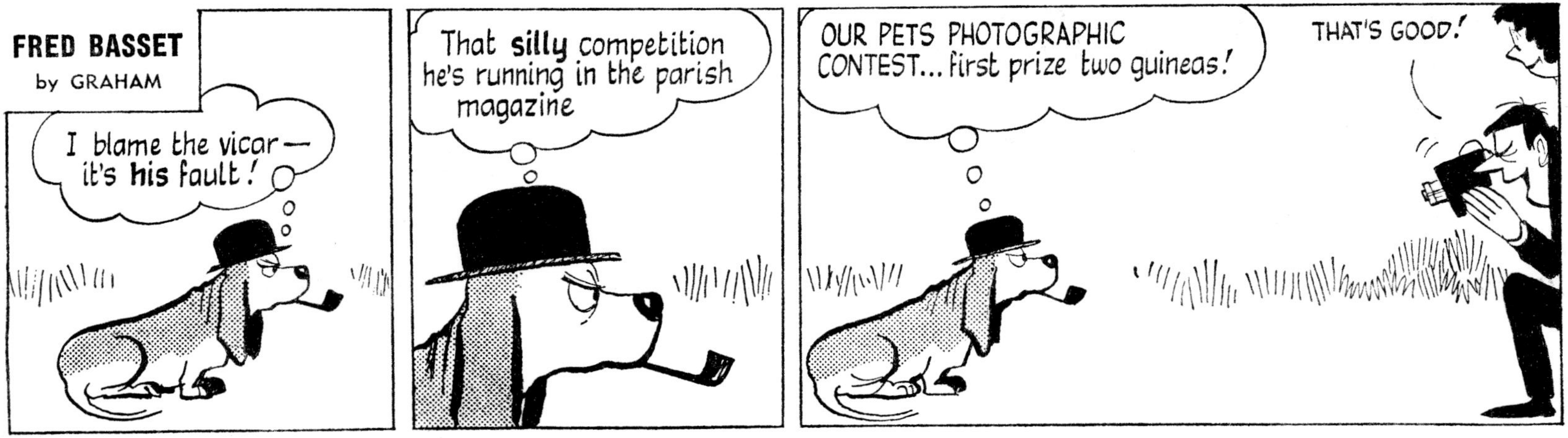
FRED BASSET
by GRAHAM
I blame the vicar— it's **his** fault!
That **silly** competition he's running in the parish magazine
OUR PETS PHOTOGRAPHIC CONTEST... first prize two guineas!
THAT'S GOOD!

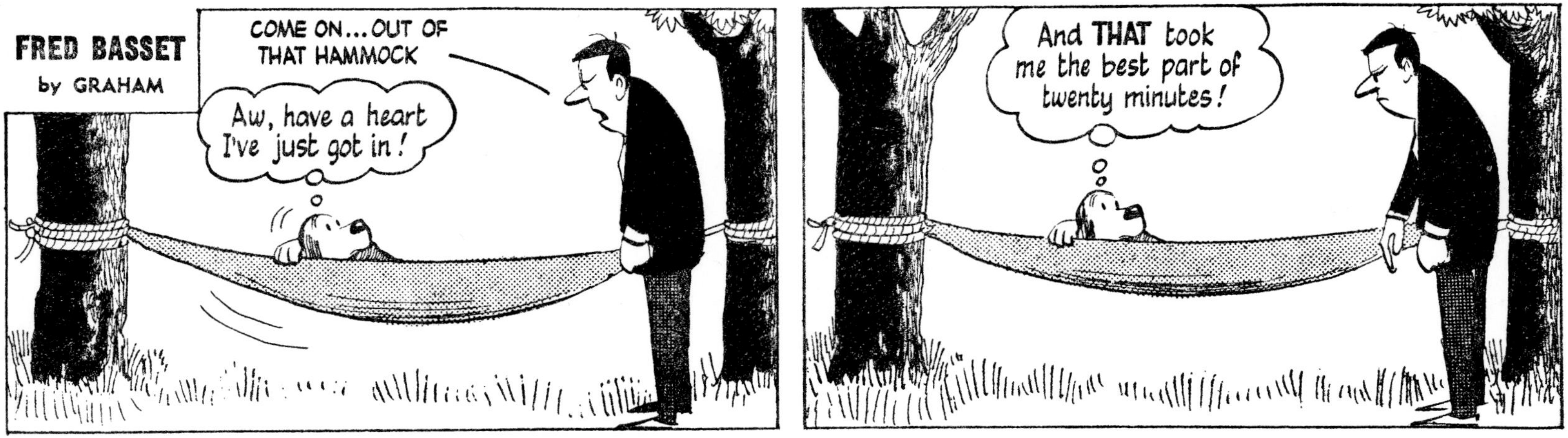
FRED BASSET
by GRAHAM
COME ON... OUT OF THAT HAMMOCK
Aw, have a heart I've just got in!
And **THAT** took me the best part of twenty minutes!

1969

FRED BASSET
by GRAHAM
HEEL!
If I'd been on my own I might've caught that rabbit!

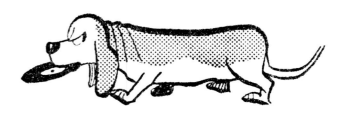

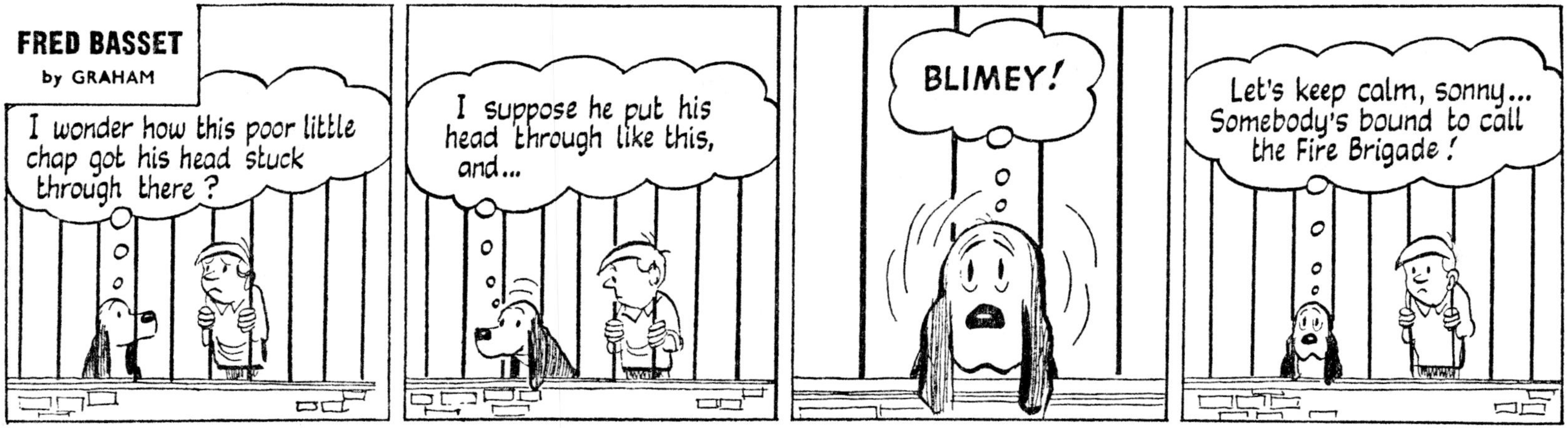
FRED BASSET
by GRAHAM
I wonder how this poor little chap got his head stuck through there?
I suppose he put his head through like this, and...
BLIMEY!
Let's keep calm, sonny... Somebody's bound to call the Fire Brigade!

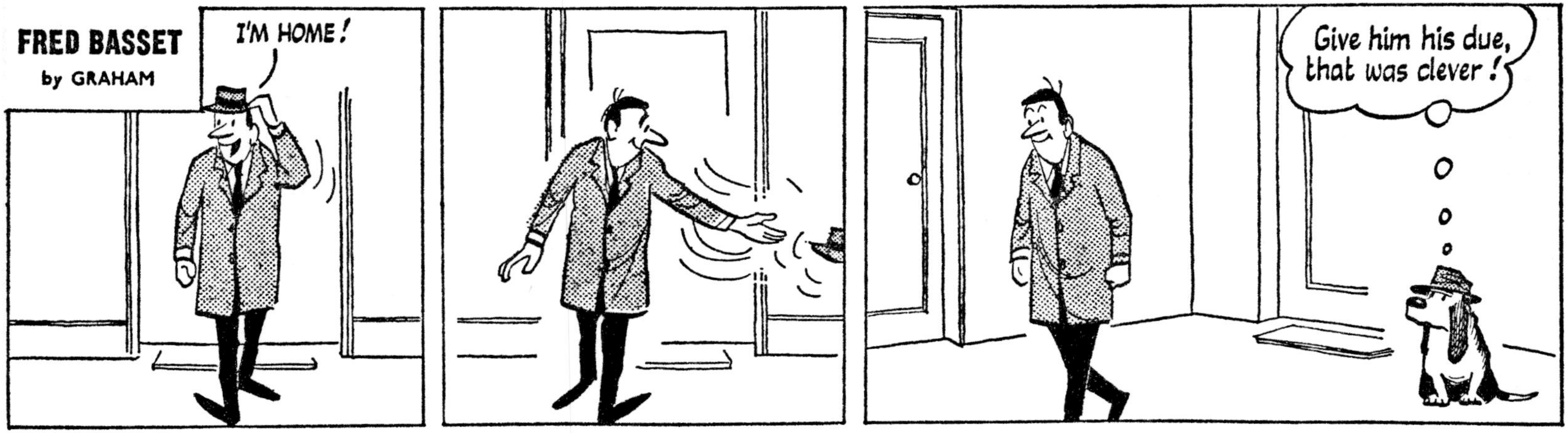
FRED BASSET
by GRAHAM
I'M HOME!
Give him his due, that was clever!

1970

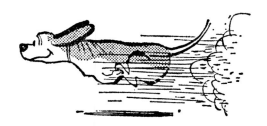

FRED BASSET
by GRAHAM

There it goes, then... Twelve o'clock... Welcome to 1970. Happy New Year!

HAPPY NEW YEAR, I don't think!

Stuck here on my own while they're enjoying themselves at the Jones's party...

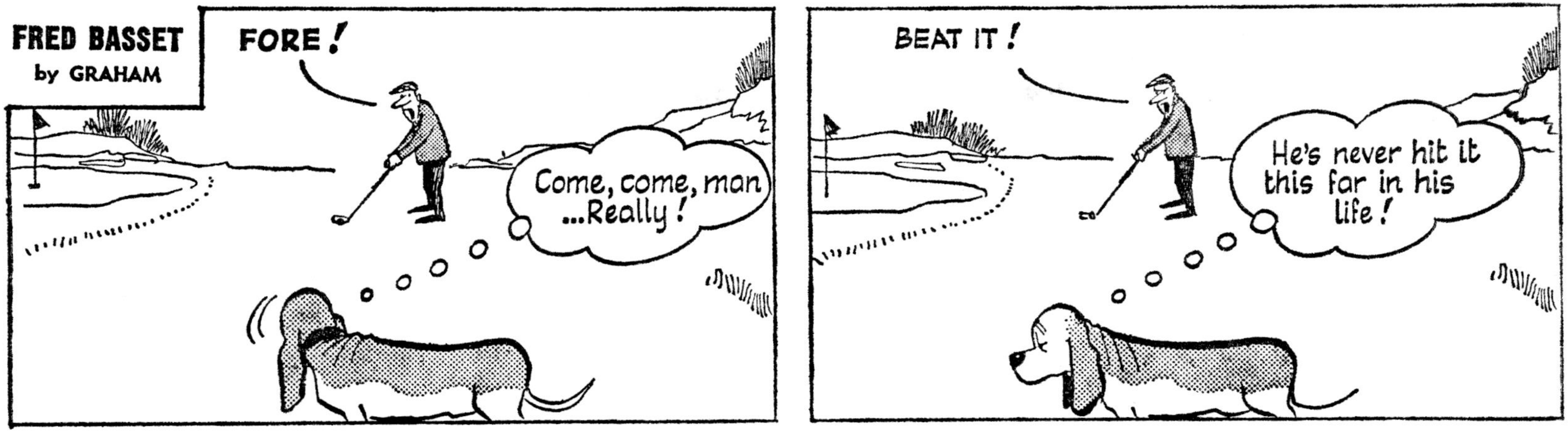
FRED BASSET
by GRAHAM
FORE!
Come, come, man ...Really!
BEAT IT!
He's never hit it this far in his life!

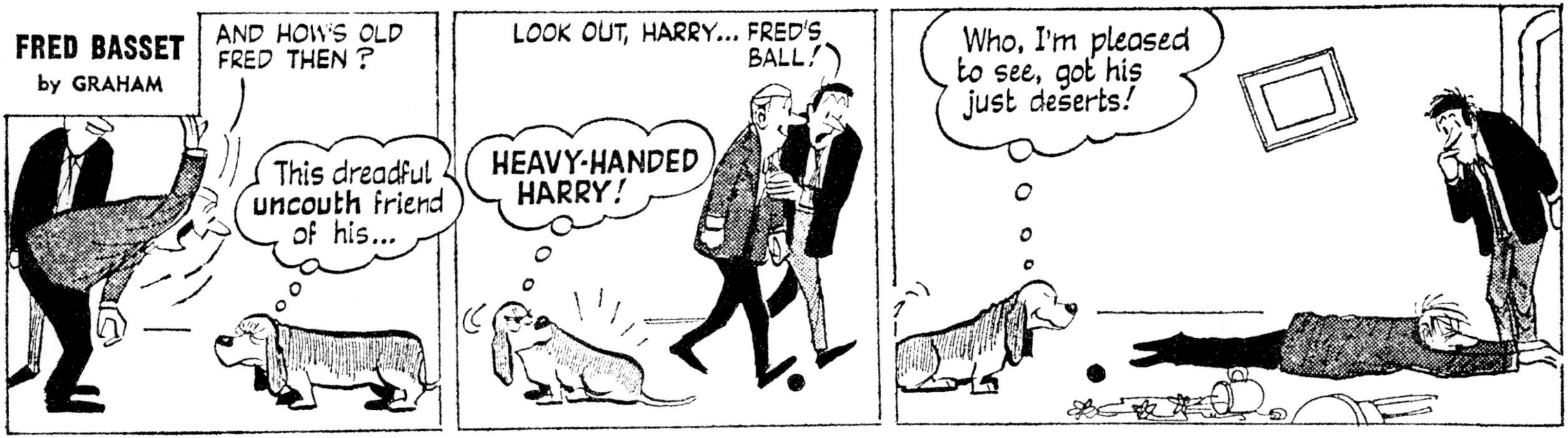
FRED BASSET
by GRAHAM
AND HOW'S OLD FRED THEN?
This dreadful uncouth friend of his...
LOOK OUT, HARRY... FRED'S BALL!
HEAVY-HANDED HARRY!
Who, I'm pleased to see, got his just deserts!

1971

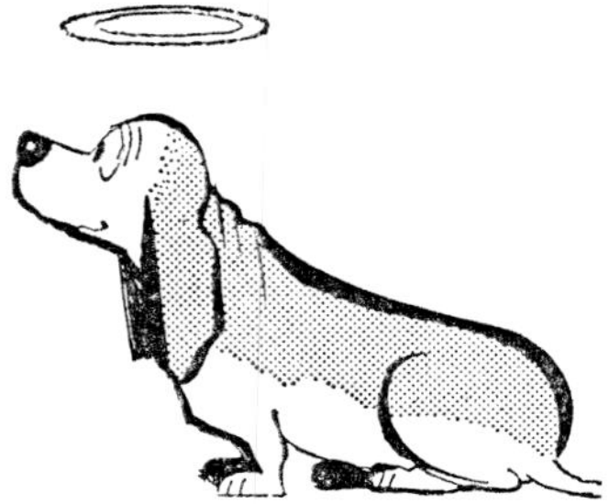

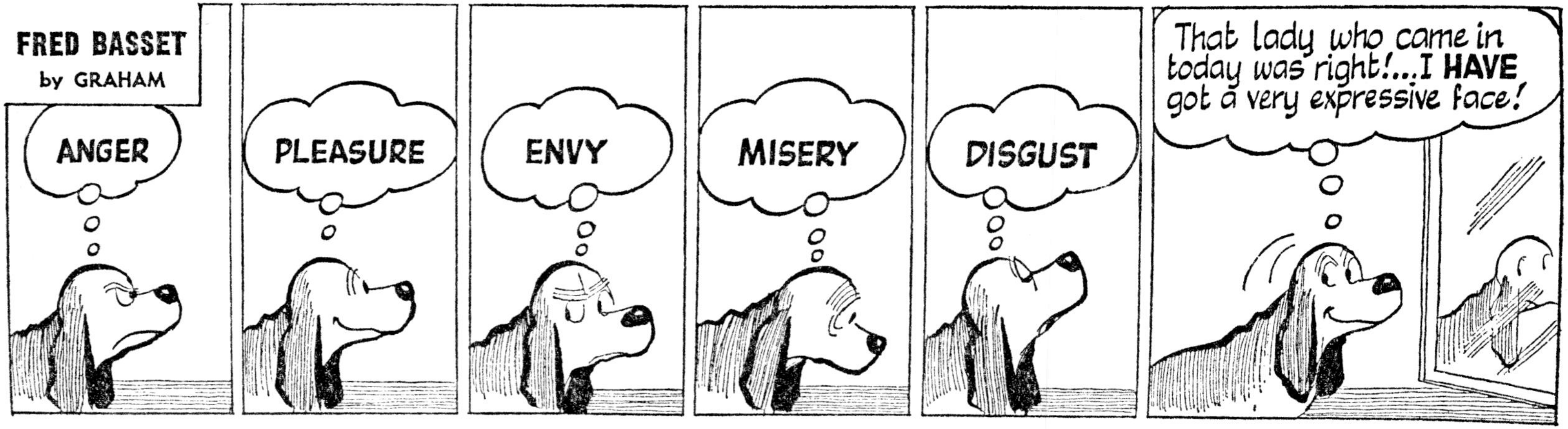
FRED BASSET
by GRAHAM
ANGER
PLEASURE
ENVY
MISERY
DISGUST
That lady who came in today was right!...I HAVE got a very expressive face!

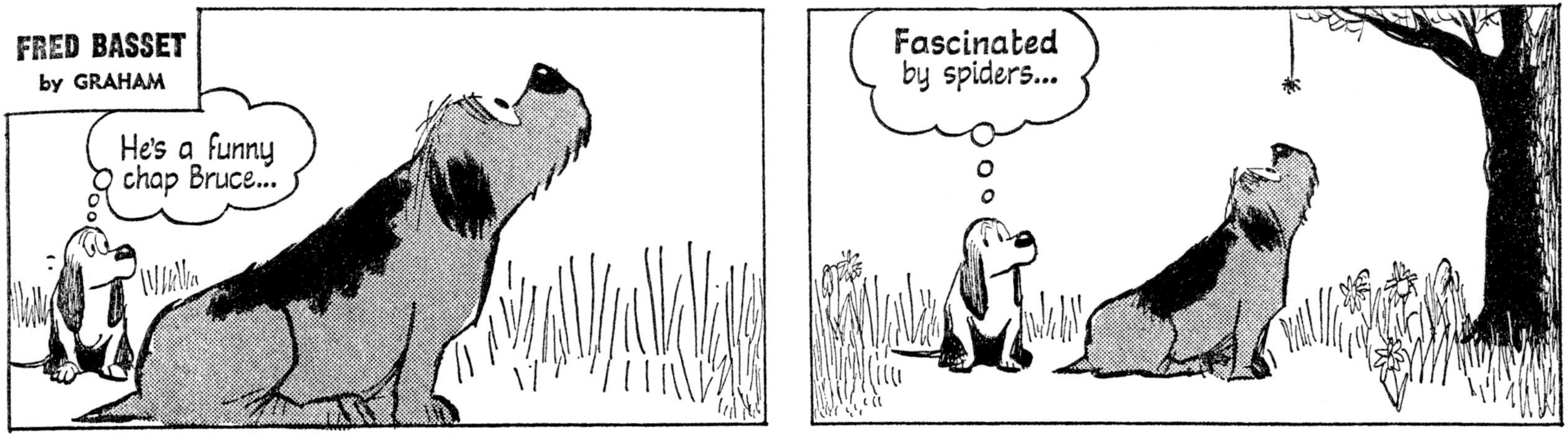
FRED BASSET
by GRAHAM
He's a funny chap Bruce...
Fascinated by spiders...

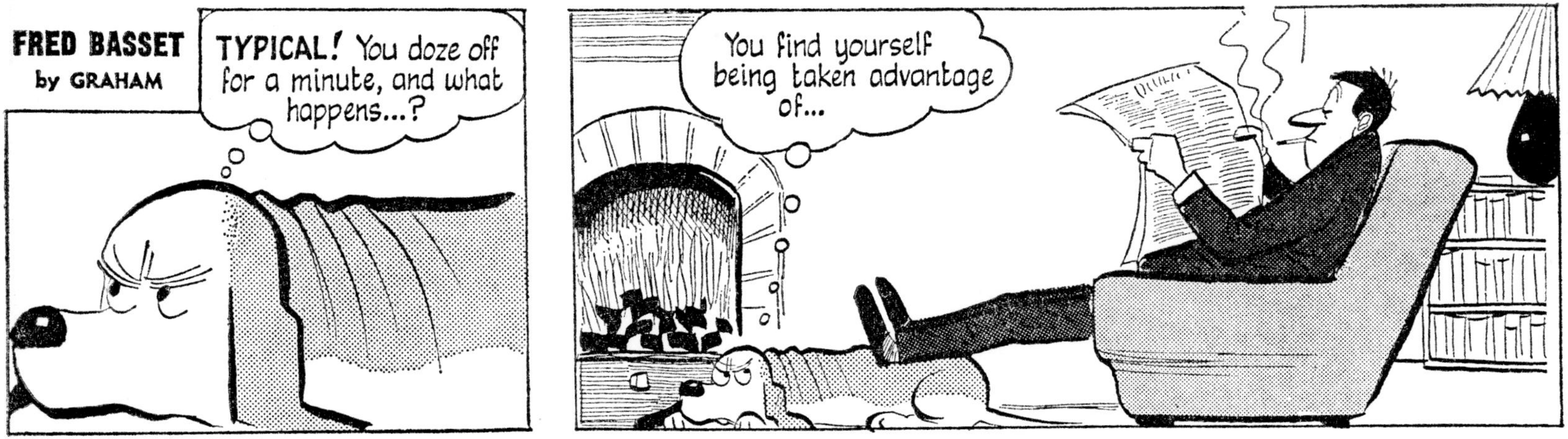
FRED BASSET
by GRAHAM
TYPICAL! You doze off for a minute, and what happens...?
You find yourself being taken advantage of...

1972

FRED BASSET
by GRAHAM
SIT!
ME NEXT!
Why, oh why am I always getting mixed up with the Tucker twins?

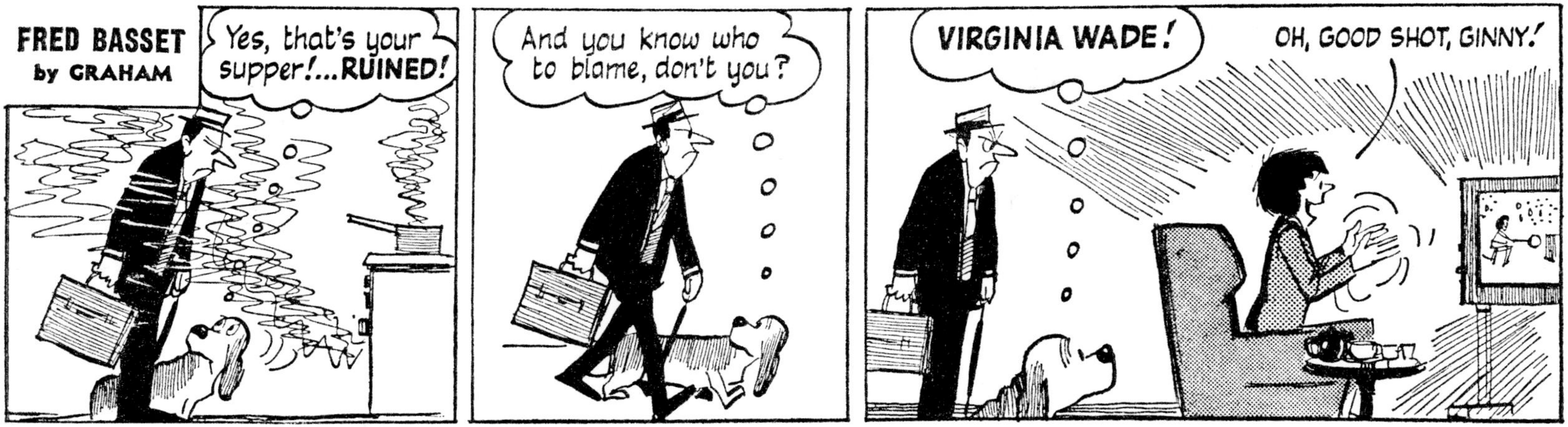
FRED BASSET
by GRAHAM
Yes, that's your supper!...RUINED!
And you know who to blame, don't you?
VIRGINIA WADE!
OH, GOOD SHOT, GINNY!

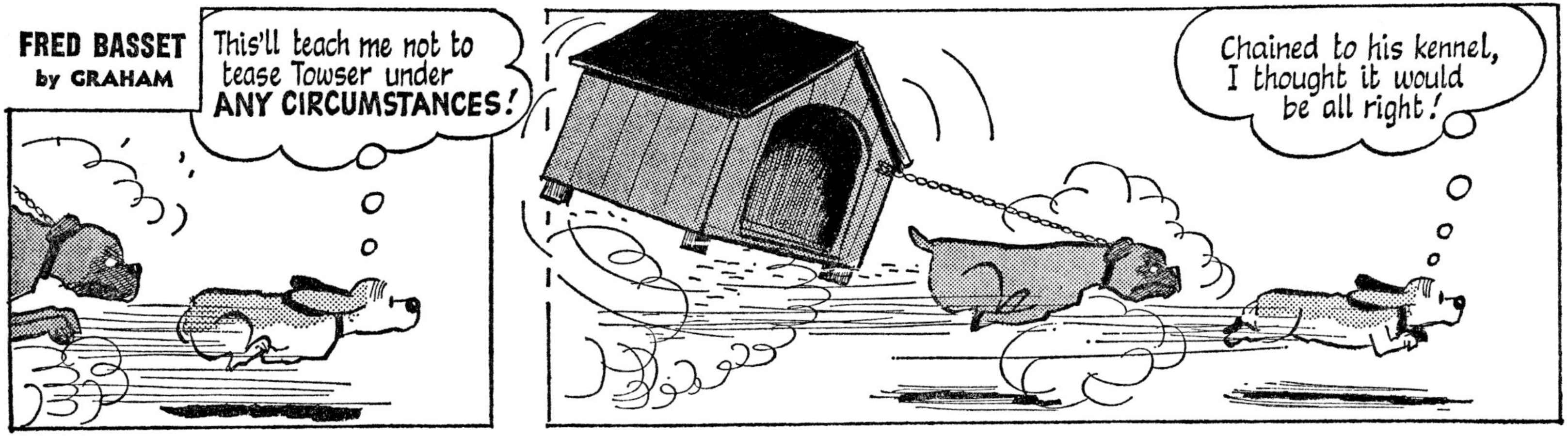
FRED BASSET
by GRAHAM
This'll teach me not to tease Towser under ANY CIRCUMSTANCES!
Chained to his kennel, I thought it would be all right!

1973

FRED BASSET
by GRAHAM
I must say, for a man of the cloth the Vicar is singularly lacking in the milk of human kindness...
CHECKMATE ONCE AGAIN, I'M AFRAID
You'd think he'd let him win occasionally!

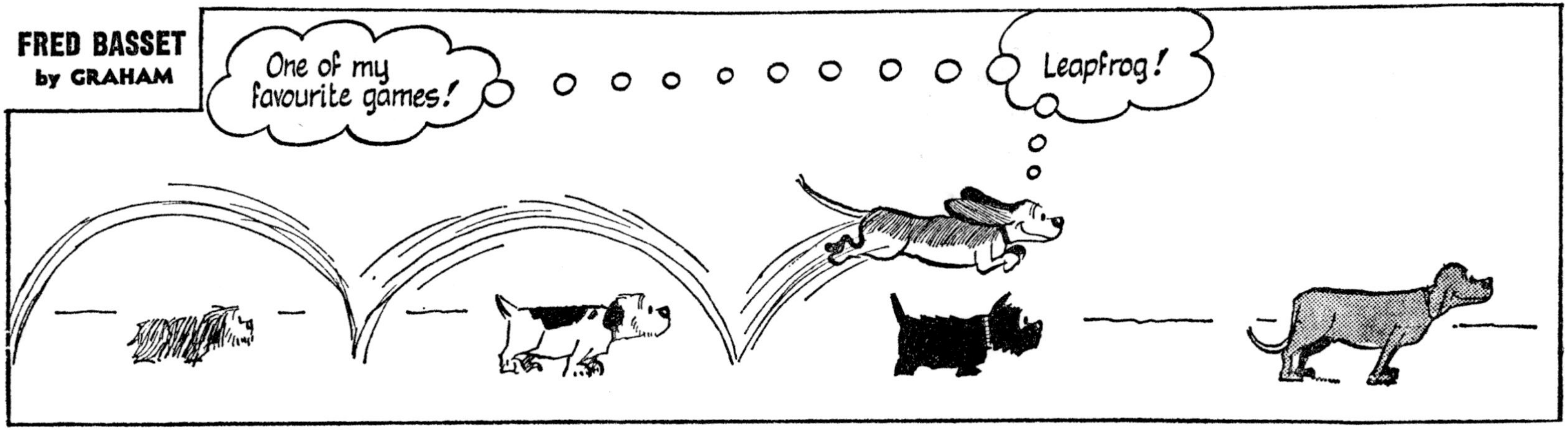
FRED BASSET
by GRAHAM
One of my favourite games!
Leapfrog!

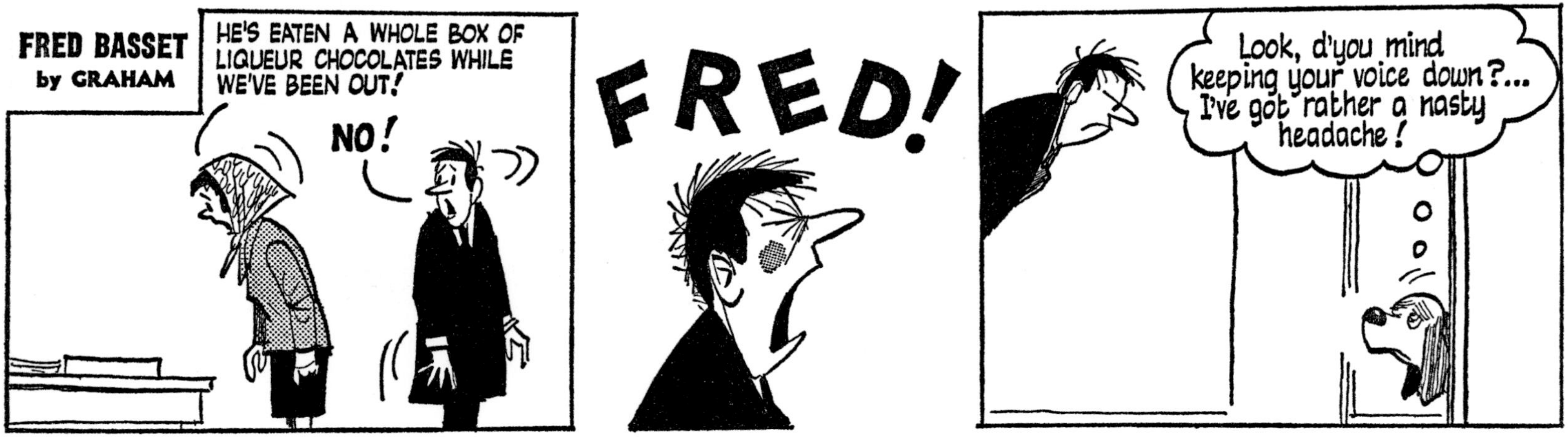
FRED BASSET
by GRAHAM
HE'S EATEN A WHOLE BOX OF LIQUEUR CHOCOLATES WHILE WE'VE BEEN OUT!
NO!
FRED!
Look, d'you mind keeping your voice down?... I've got rather a nasty headache!

1974

FRED BASSET
by GRAHAM

Here come two of our most respected senior citizens... and looking remarkably spry for their years!

Considering Mr. Gibson's over eighty...

...and Spot must be getting on for fourteen...

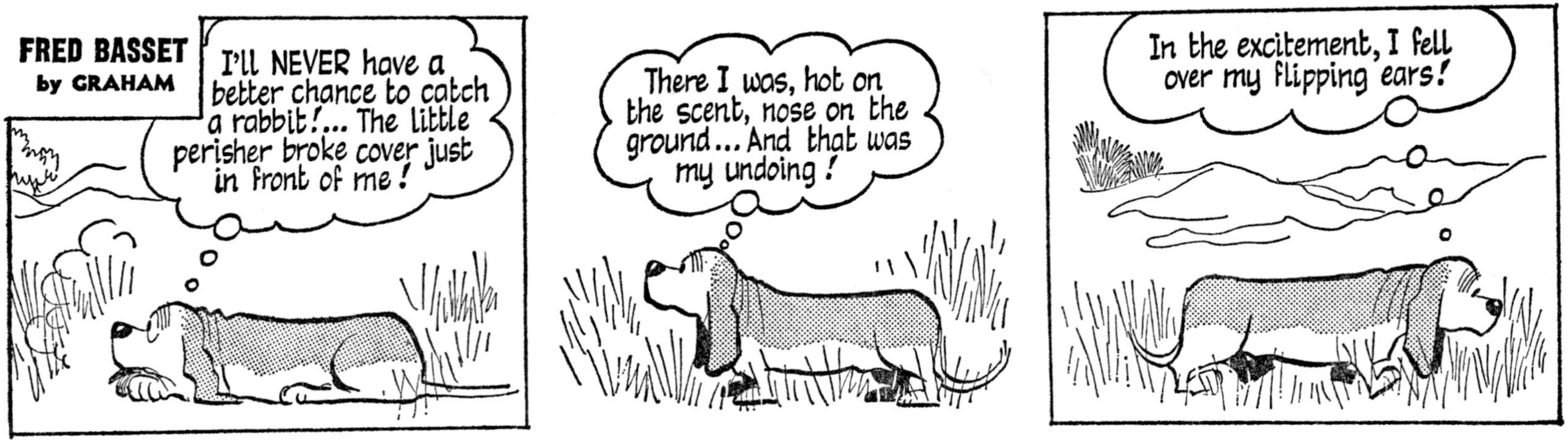
FRED BASSET
by GRAHAM
I'll NEVER have a better chance to catch a rabbit!... The little perisher broke cover just in front of me!
There I was, hot on the scent, nose on the ground... And that was my undoing!
In the excitement, I fell over my flipping ears!

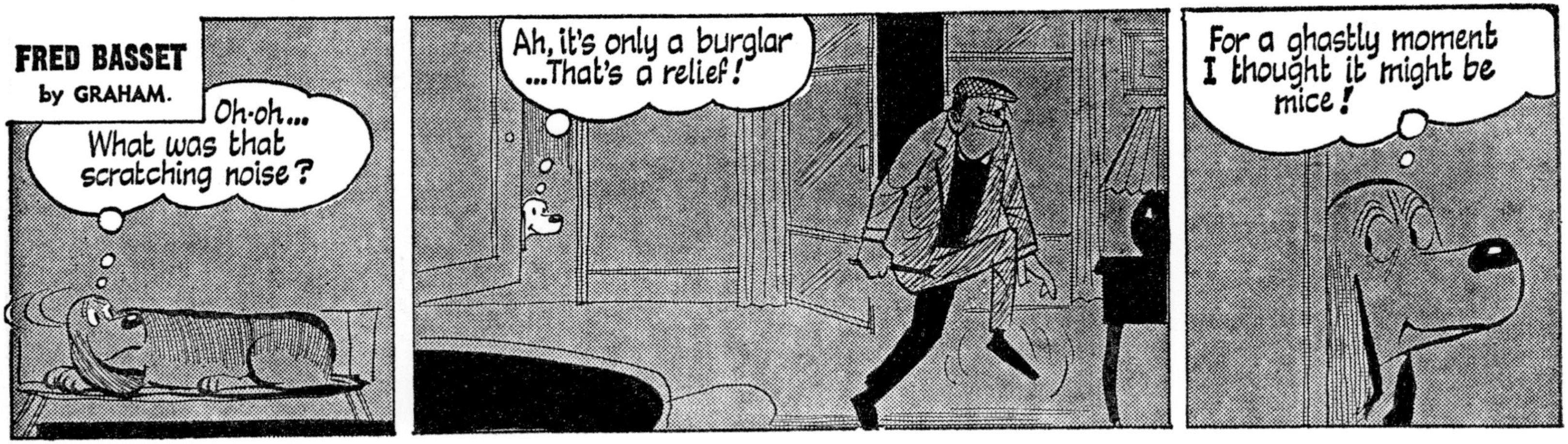
FRED BASSET
by GRAHAM.
Oh-oh... What was that scratching noise?
Ah, it's only a burglar ...That's a relief!
For a ghastly moment I thought it might be mice!

1975

FRED BASSET
by GRAHAM

SHAKESPEARE REFERRED TO BASSETS, APPARENTLY...
"Their heads hung with ears that sweep away the morning dew; crook-kneed and dew lapped... slow in pursuit"...

Cheek!

Who is this fellow Shakespeare, anyway?

CELEBRATING **50** YEARS

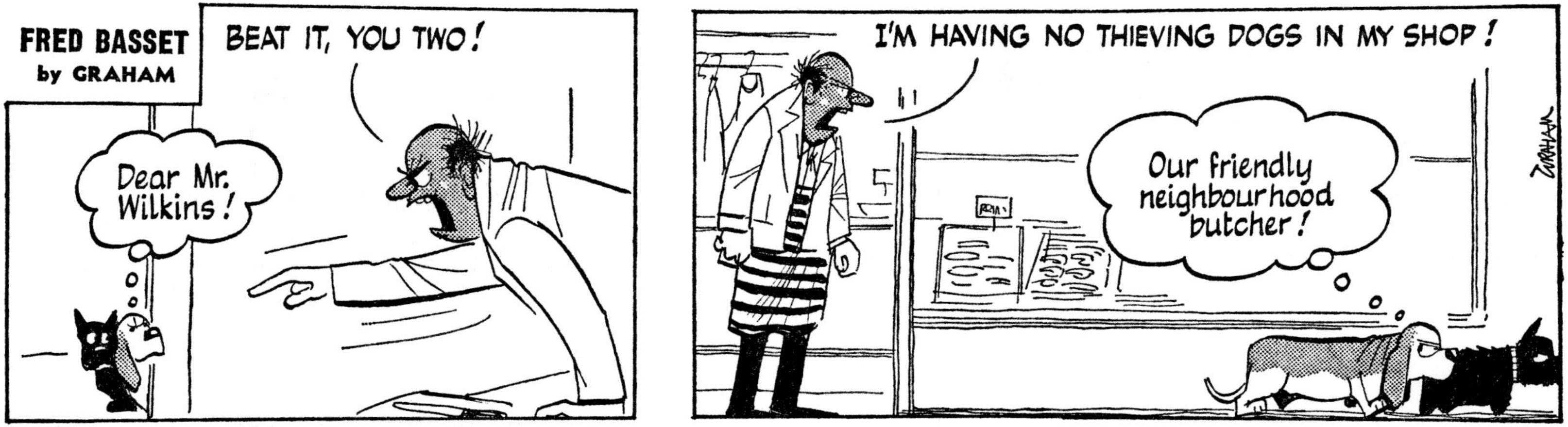
FRED BASSET
by GRAHAM
BEAT IT, YOU TWO!
Dear Mr. Wilkins!
I'M HAVING NO THIEVING DOGS IN MY SHOP!
Our friendly neighbourhood butcher!

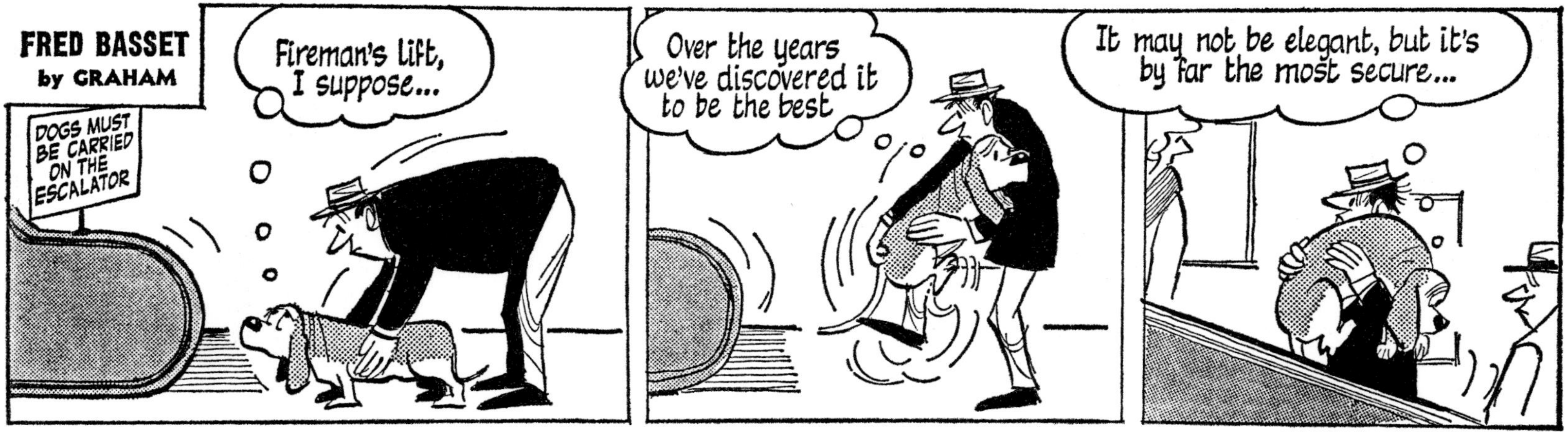
FRED BASSET
by GRAHAM
DOGS MUST BE CARRIED ON THE ESCALATOR
Fireman's lift, I suppose...
Over the years we've discovered it to be the best
It may not be elegant, but it's by far the most secure...

1976

FRED BASSET
by GRAHAM
So far, so good... Six down, "A man's name." Four letters. Third letter E... FRED!
No, it can't be Fred... That's a dog's name
Abel?... Greg?... Drew? ...Alex?...
GRAHAM

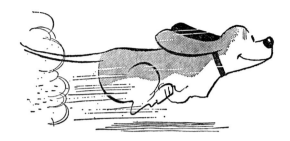

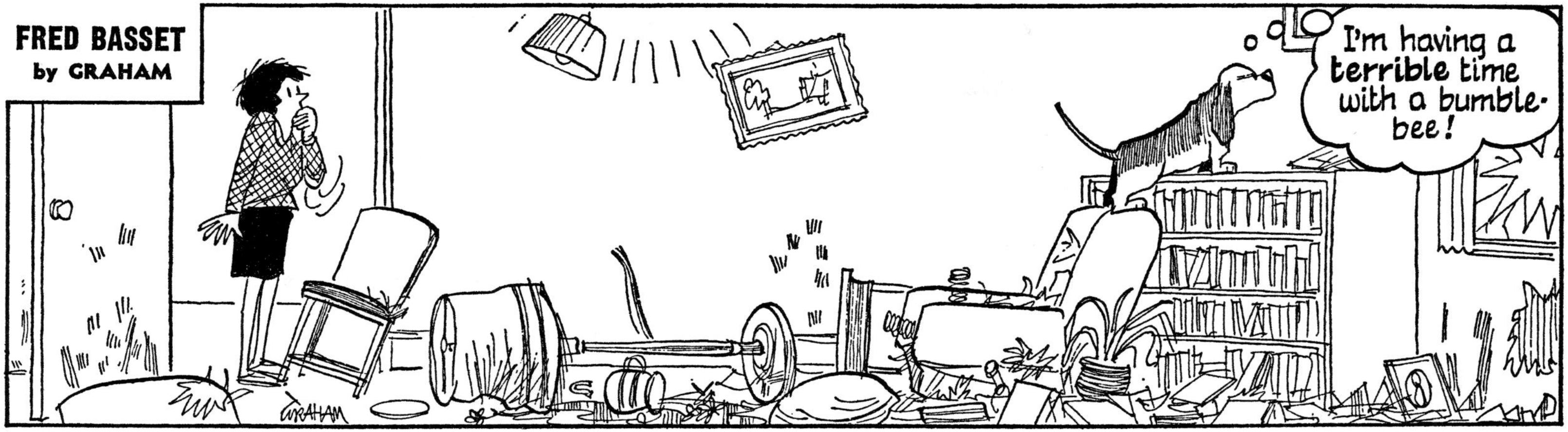
FRED BASSET
by GRAHAM
I'm having a terrible time with a bumble-bee!
GRAHAM

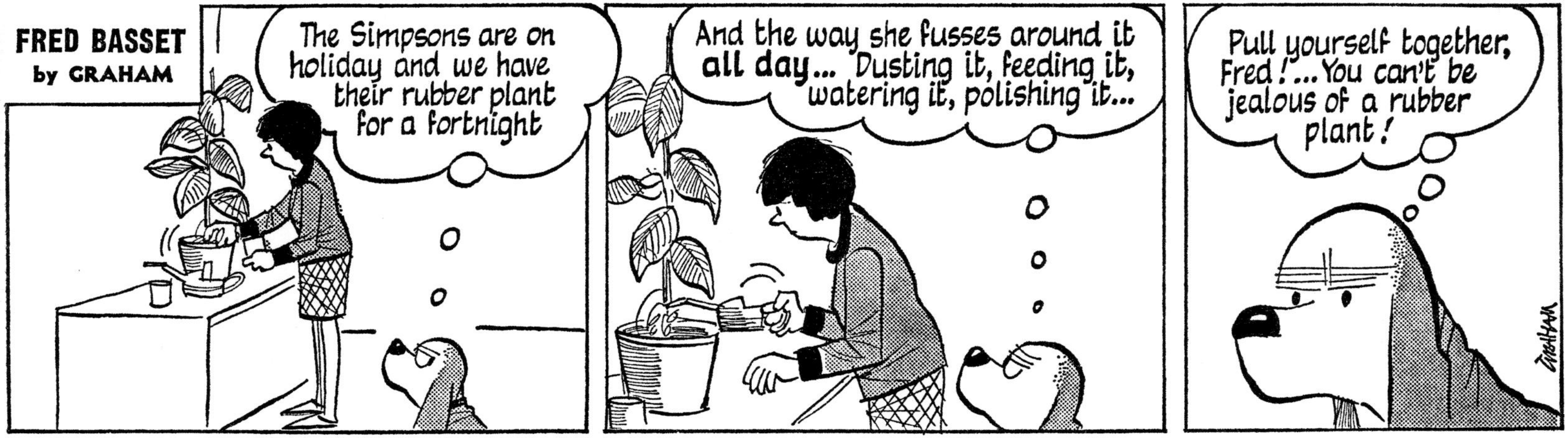
FRED BASSET
by GRAHAM
The Simpsons are on holiday and we have their rubber plant for a fortnight
And the way she fusses around it all day... Dusting it, feeding it, watering it, polishing it...
Pull yourself together, Fred!...You can't be jealous of a rubber plant!
GRAHAM

1977

FRED BASSET
by GRAHAM
Always the same when it comes to the gardening season...
I never get a proper walk !
GRAHAM

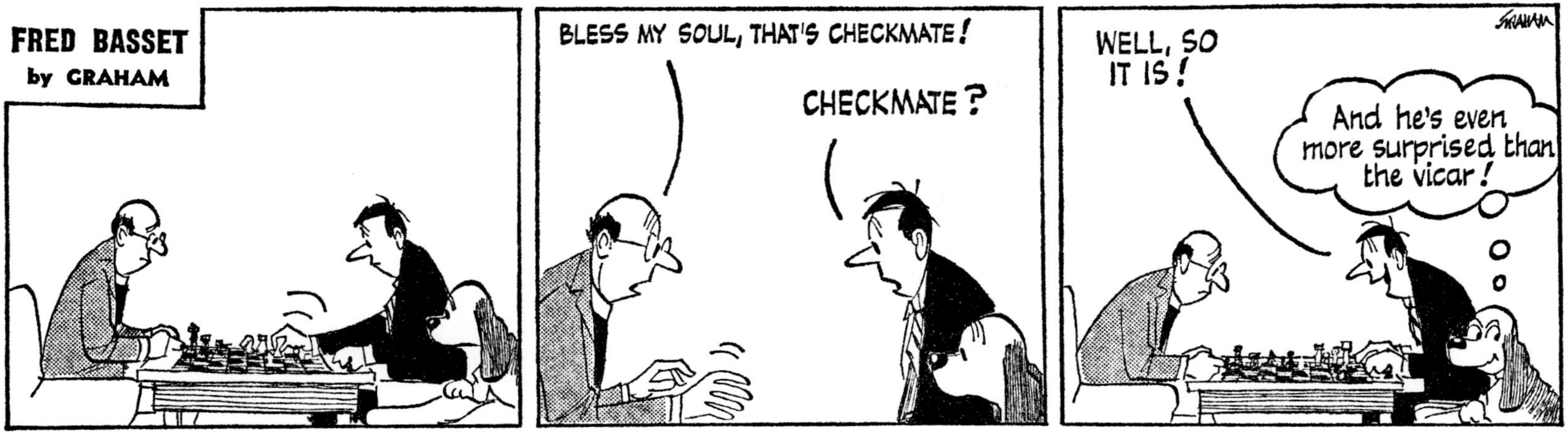
FRED BASSET
by GRAHAM
BLESS MY SOUL, THAT'S CHECKMATE!
CHECKMATE?
WELL, SO IT IS!
And he's even more surprised than the vicar!
GRAHAM

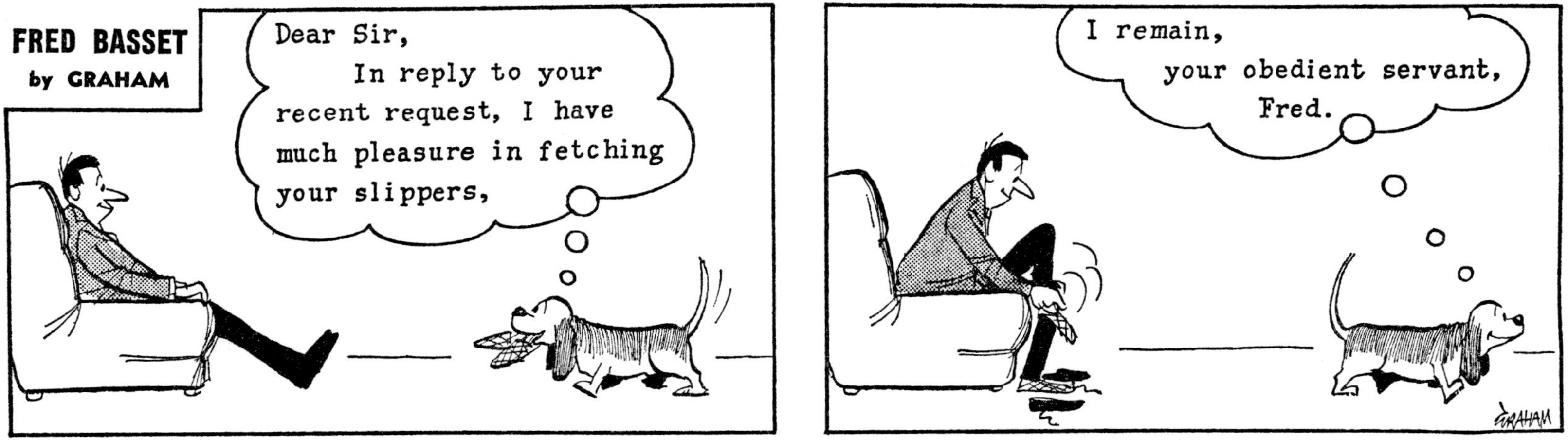
FRED BASSET
by GRAHAM
Dear Sir,
In reply to your recent request, I have much pleasure in fetching your slippers,
I remain,
your obedient servant,
Fred.
GRAHAM

1978

FRED BASSET
by GRAHAM
WE'LL HAVE THIS ONE...
DOG COATS
Tartan!... I like it!
Fred MacBasset!
GRAHAM

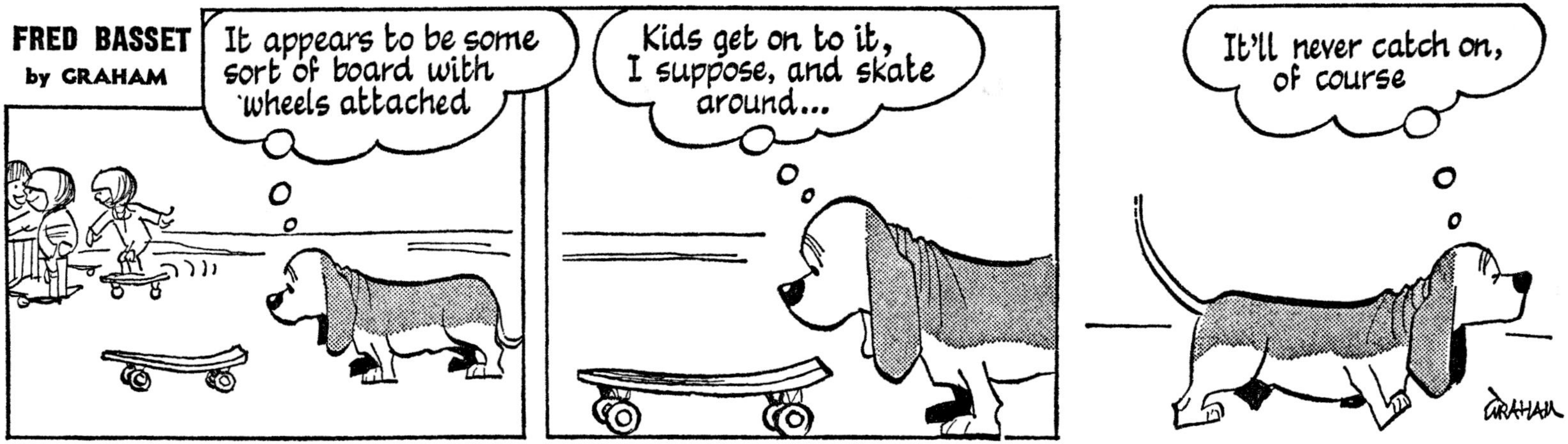
FRED BASSET
by GRAHAM
It appears to be some sort of board with wheels attached
Kids get on to it, I suppose, and skate around...
It'll never catch on, of course
GRAHAM

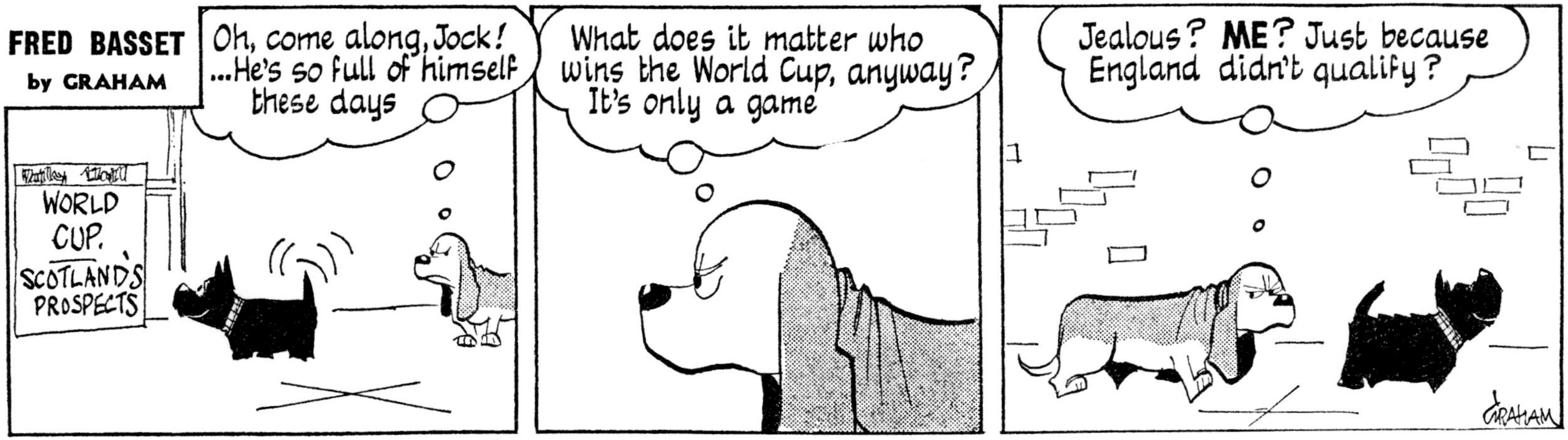
FRED BASSET
by GRAHAM
WORLD CUP. SCOTLAND'S PROSPECTS
Oh, come along, Jock! ...He's so full of himself these days
What does it matter who wins the World Cup, anyway? It's only a game
Jealous? ME? Just because England didn't qualify?
GRAHAM

1979

FRED BASSET
by GRAHAM
I've seen some bones in my time, but this is FANTASTIC!
The shin bone of a brontosaurus?
GRAHAM

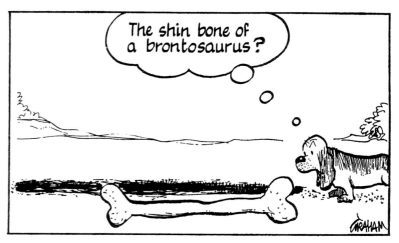

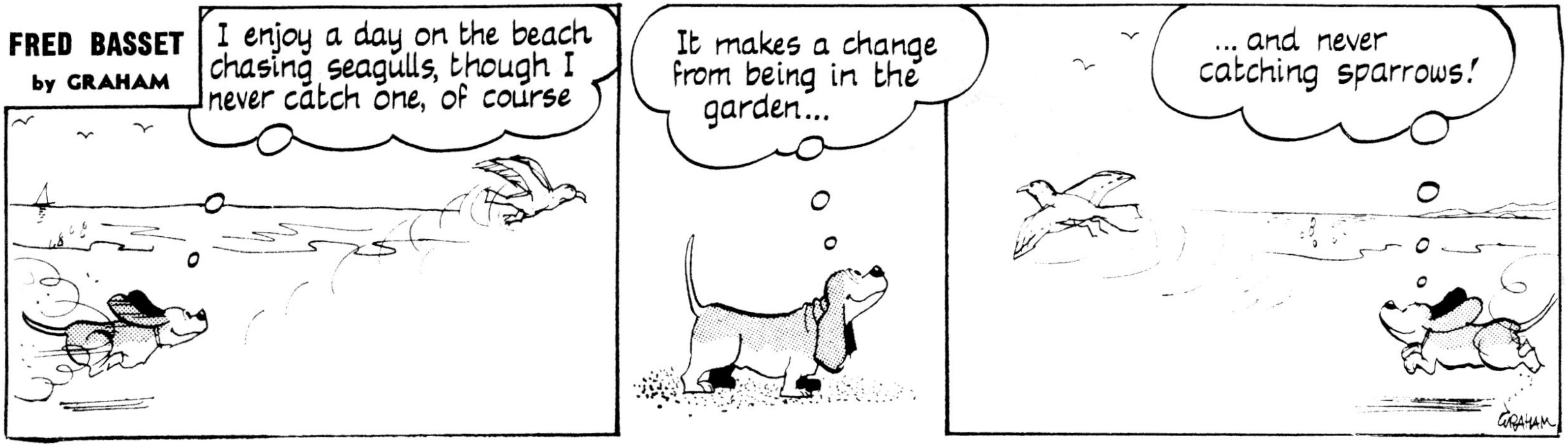
FRED BASSET
by GRAHAM
I enjoy a day on the beach chasing seagulls, though I never catch one, of course
It makes a change from being in the garden...
... and never catching sparrows!
GRAHAM

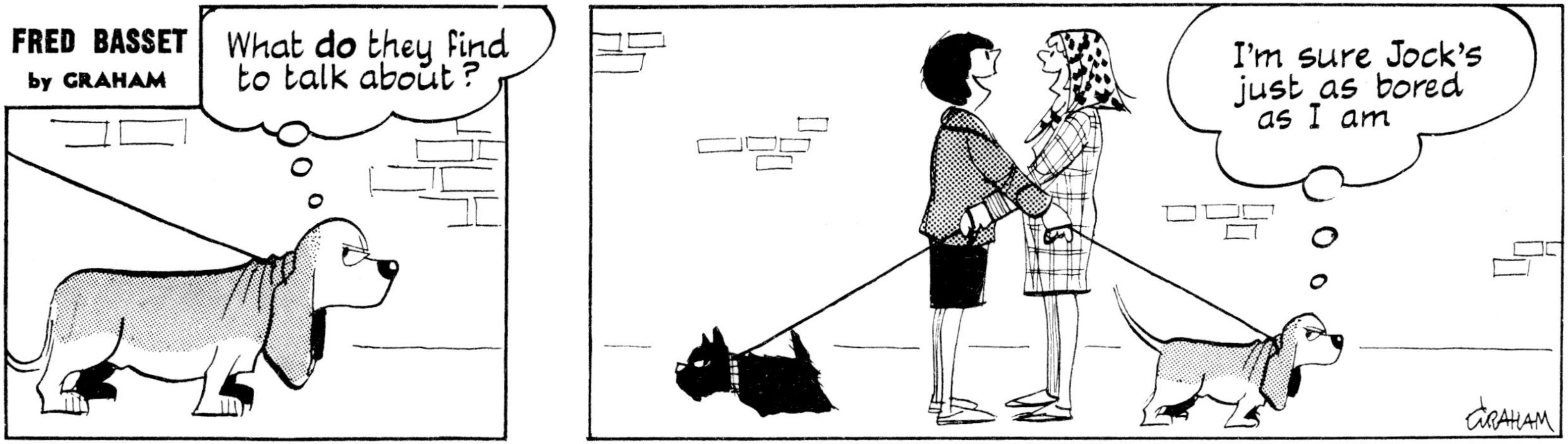
FRED BASSET
by GRAHAM
What do they find to talk about?
I'm sure Jock's just as bored as I am
GRAHAM

1980

FRED BASSET
by GRAHAM
As if I don't have enough trouble with the little perishers in the garden
CUCKOO
Missed it!
GRAHAM

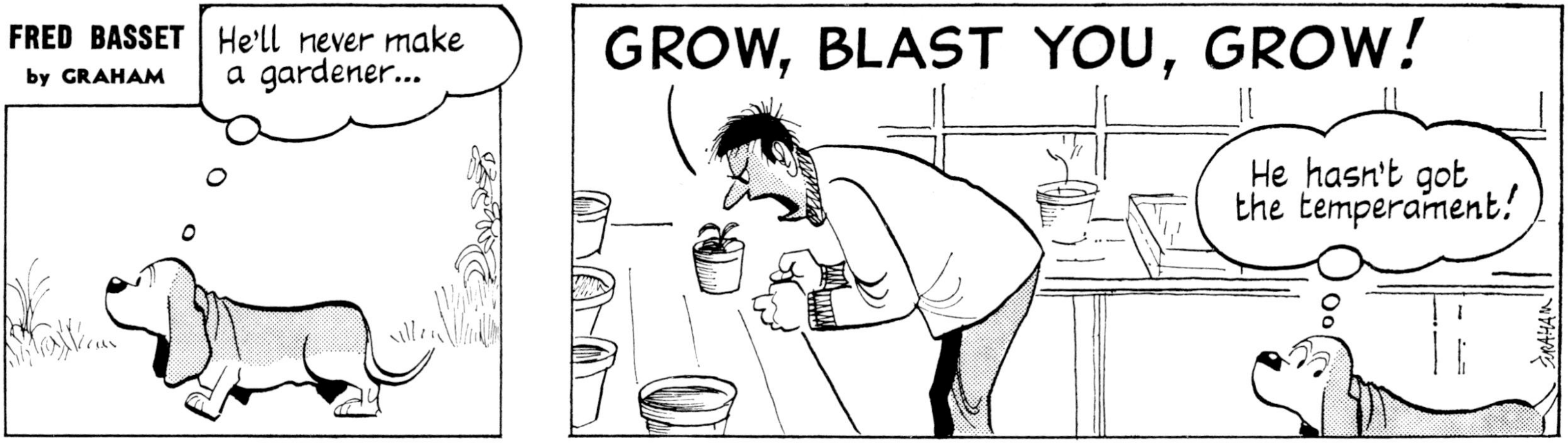
FRED BASSET
by GRAHAM
He'll never make a gardener...
GROW, BLAST YOU, GROW!
He hasn't got the temperament!
GRAHAM

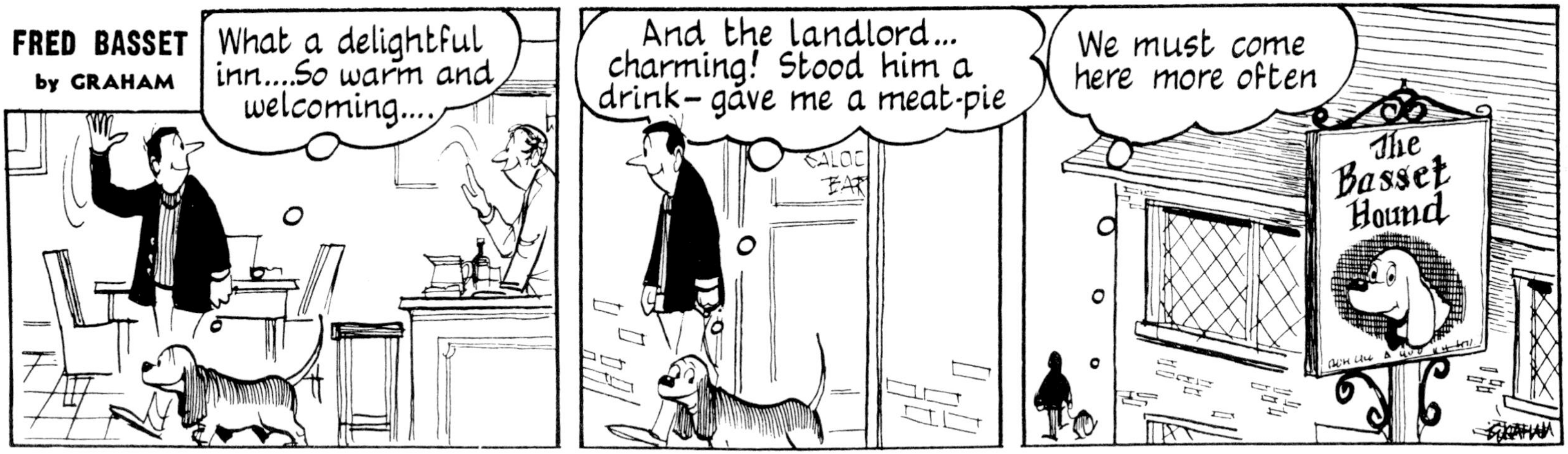
FRED BASSET
by GRAHAM
What a delightful inn....So warm and welcoming....
And the landlord... charming! Stood him a drink– gave me a meat-pie
We must come here more often
The Basset Hound
GRAHAM

1981

FRED BASSET by GRAHAM

AH!...I SEE THE NEW PEOPLE OPPOSITE HAVE A WHITE SALUKI

Shame on them!

Why can't they be like us and have a British car?

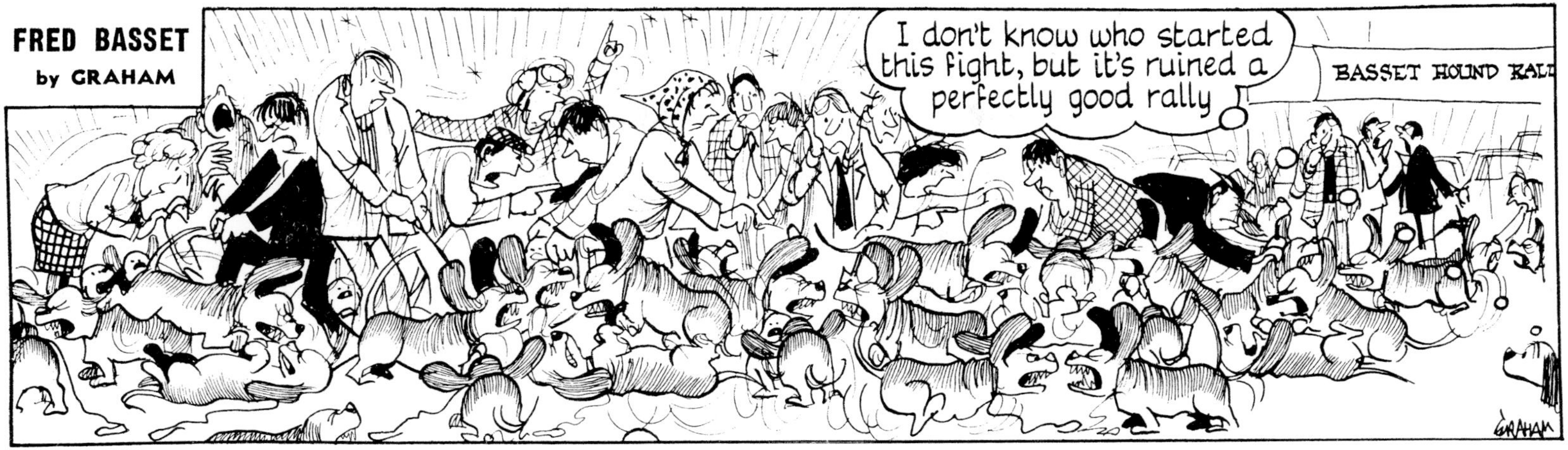
FRED BASSET
by GRAHAM
I don't know who started this fight, but it's ruined a perfectly good rally
BASSET HOUND RALL
GRAHAM

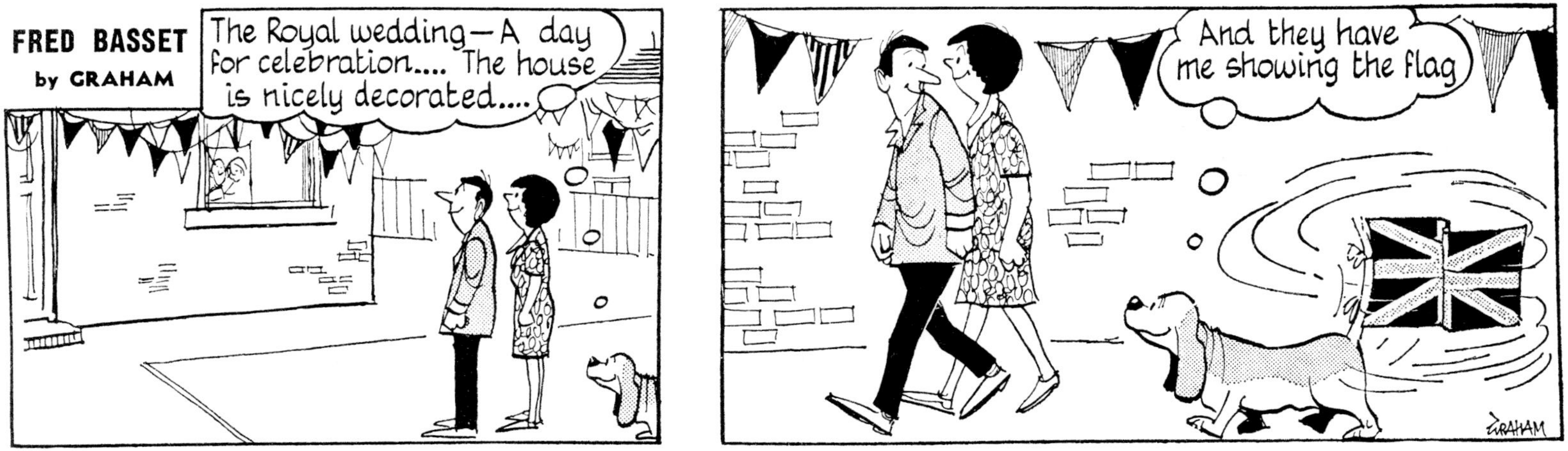
FRED BASSET
by GRAHAM
The Royal wedding—A day for celebration.... The house is nicely decorated....
And they have me showing the flag
GRAHAM

1982

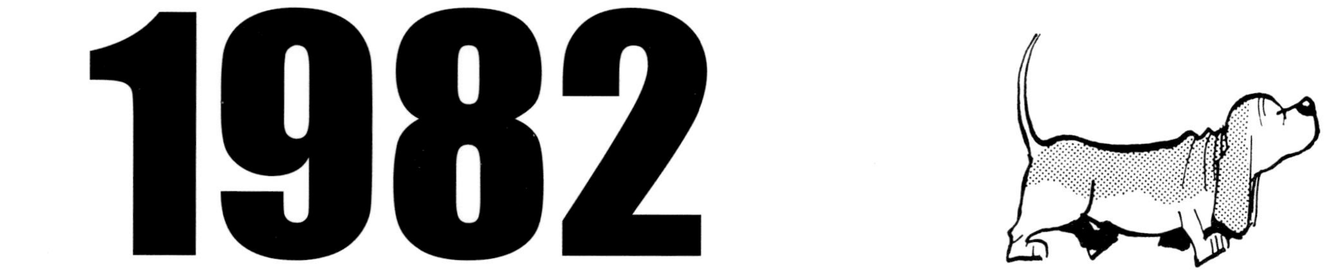

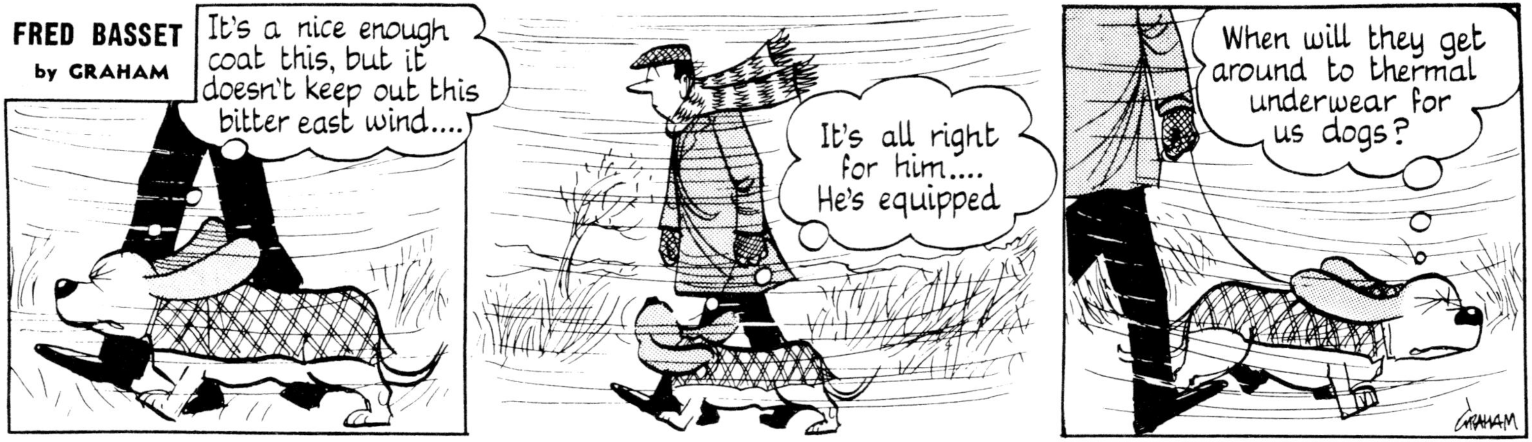
FRED BASSET
by GRAHAM
It's a nice enough coat this, but it doesn't keep out this bitter east wind....
It's all right for him.... He's equipped
When will they get around to thermal underwear for us dogs?
GRAHAM

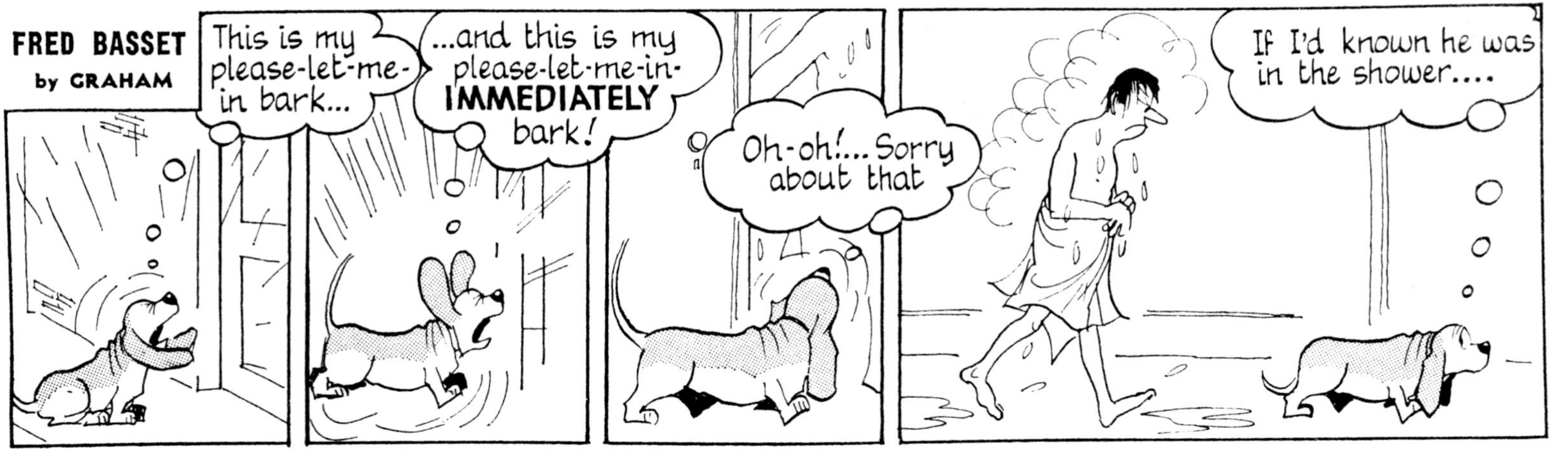
FRED BASSET
by GRAHAM
This is my please-let-me-in bark...
...and this is my please-let-me-in-IMMEDIATELY bark!
Oh-oh!... Sorry about that
If I'd known he was in the shower....

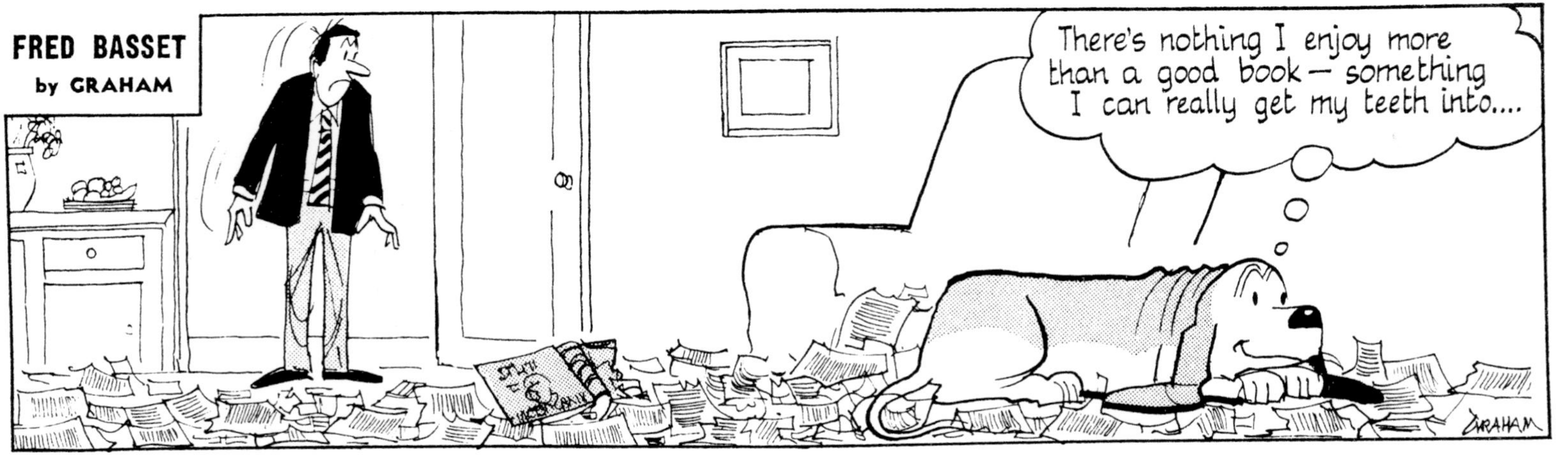
FRED BASSET
by GRAHAM
There's nothing I enjoy more than a good book – something I can really get my teeth into....
GRAHAM

1983

FRED BASSET
by GRAHAM
The whistle!
Coming!
When did they buy this thing?
GRAHAM

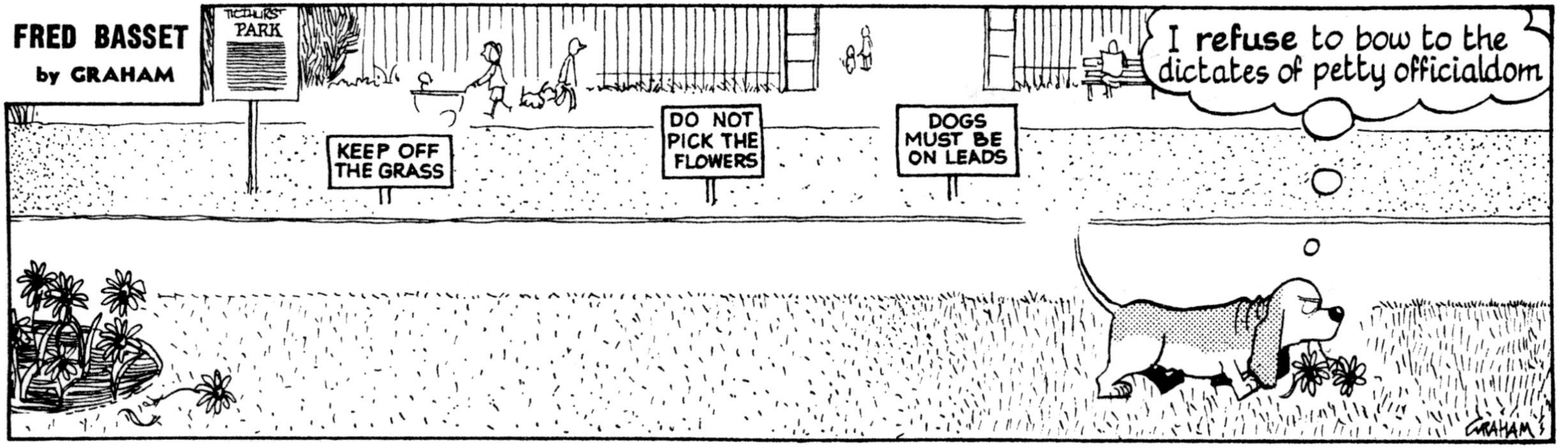
FRED BASSET
by GRAHAM
PARK
KEEP OFF THE GRASS
DO NOT PICK THE FLOWERS
DOGS MUST BE ON LEADS
I **refuse** to bow to the dictates of petty officialdom
GRAHAM

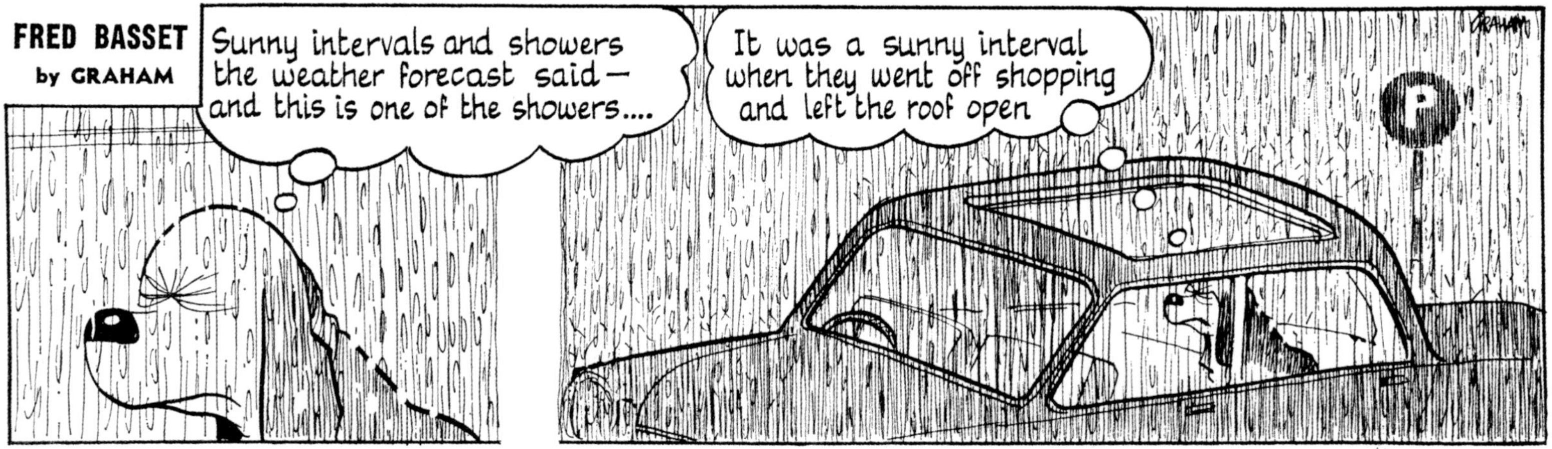
FRED BASSET
by GRAHAM
Sunny intervals and showers the weather forecast said— and this is one of the showers....
It was a sunny interval when they went off shopping and left the roof open
P
GRAHAM

1984

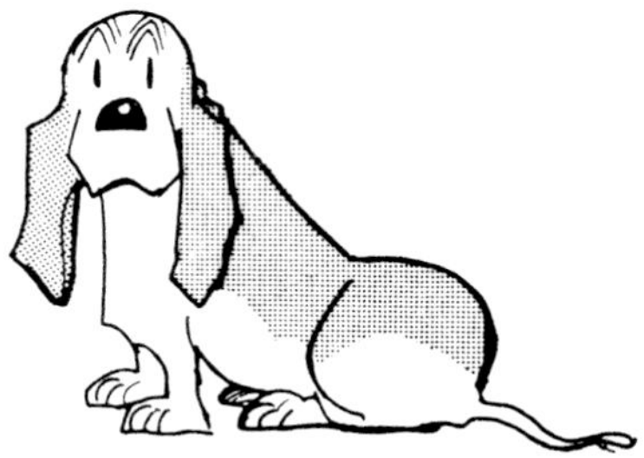

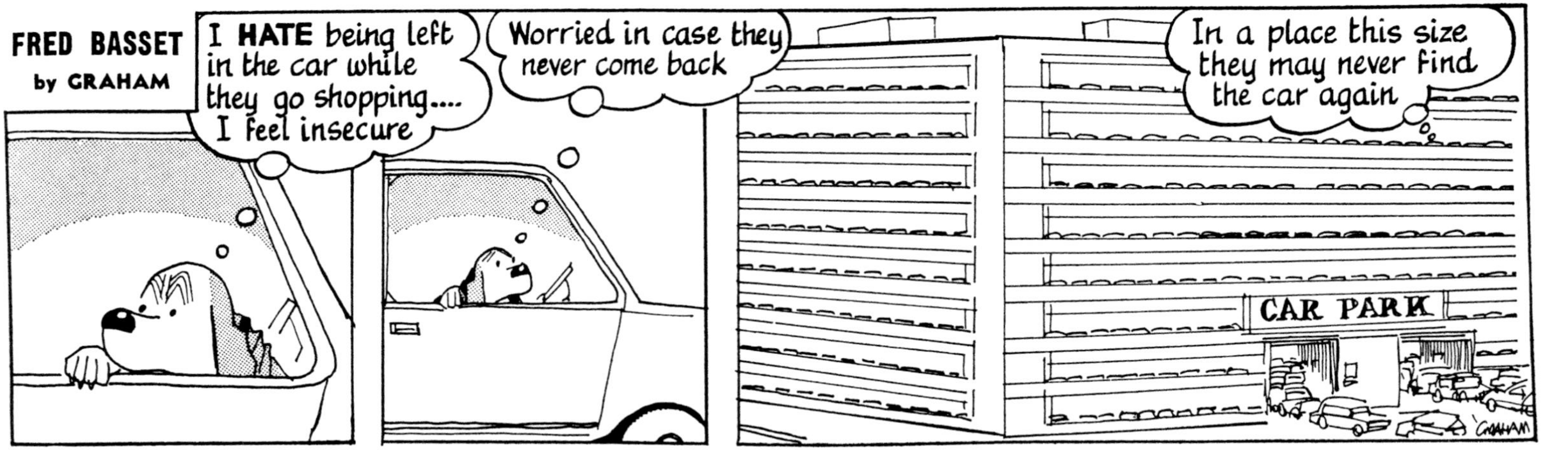
FRED BASSET
by GRAHAM
I HATE being left in the car while they go shopping.... I feel insecure
Worried in case they never come back
In a place this size they may never find the car again
CAR PARK
GRAHAM

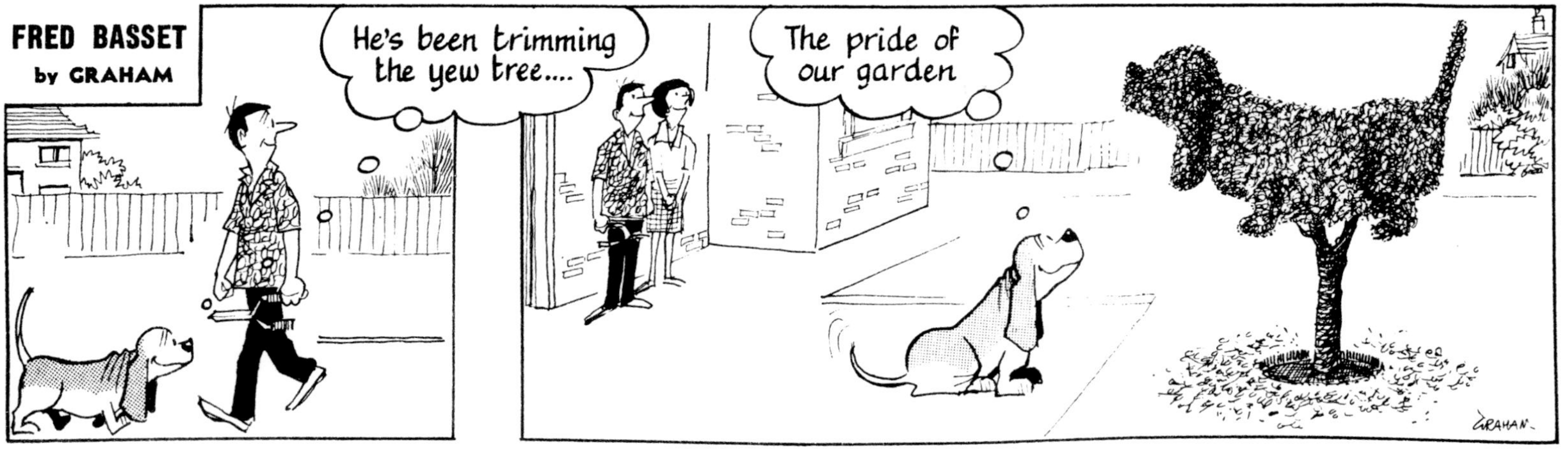
FRED BASSET
by GRAHAM
He's been trimming the yew tree....
The pride of our garden
GRAHAM

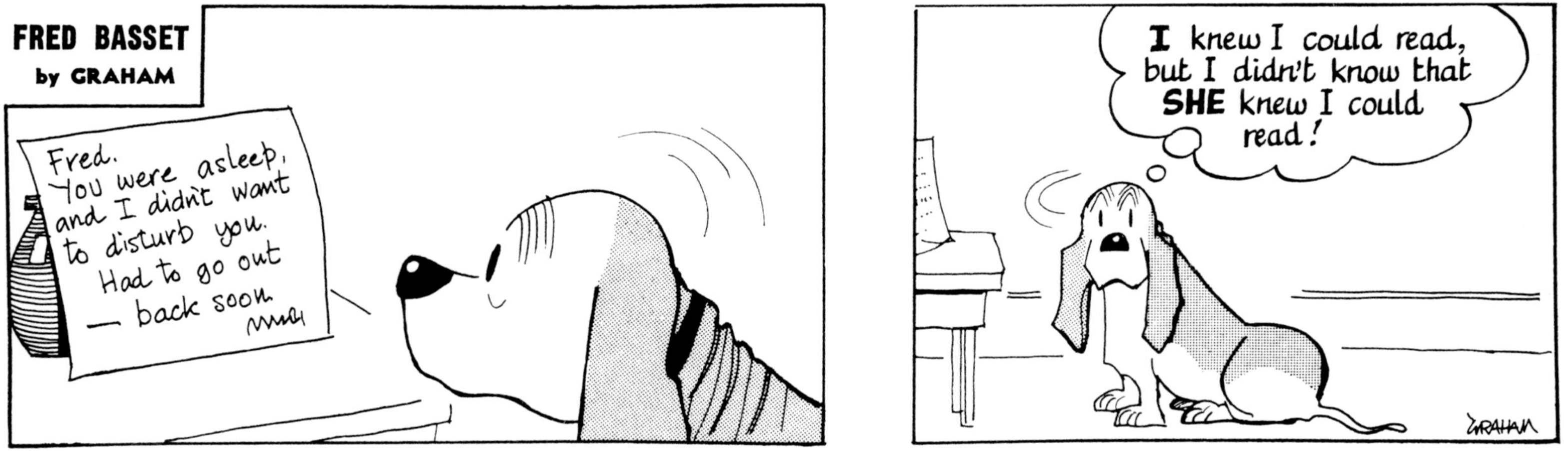
FRED BASSET
by GRAHAM
Fred.
You were asleep,
and I didn't want
to disturb you.
Had to go out
— back soon
I knew I could read, but I didn't know that SHE knew I could read!
GRAHAM

1985

FRED BASSET
by GRAHAM
One of his fishing stories I suppose! The one that got away.
ABOUT THIS LENGTH...BROWN AND WHITE... ANSWERS TO THE NAME OF FRED...
ISN'T THAT HIM THERE ?
WELL, SO IT IS! I THOUGHT I'D LOST YOU, FRED
I misjudged him!
GRAHAM

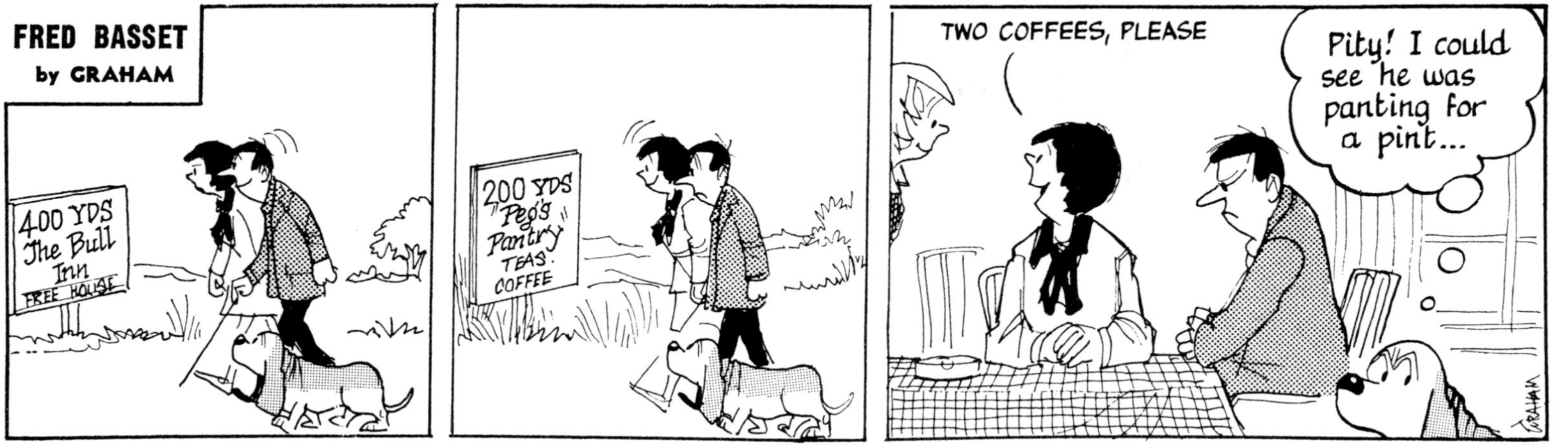
FRED BASSET
by GRAHAM
400 YDS The Bull Inn
FREE HOUSE
200 YDS "Peg's Pantry" TEAS COFFEE
TWO COFFEES, PLEASE
Pity! I could see he was panting for a pint...
GRAHAM

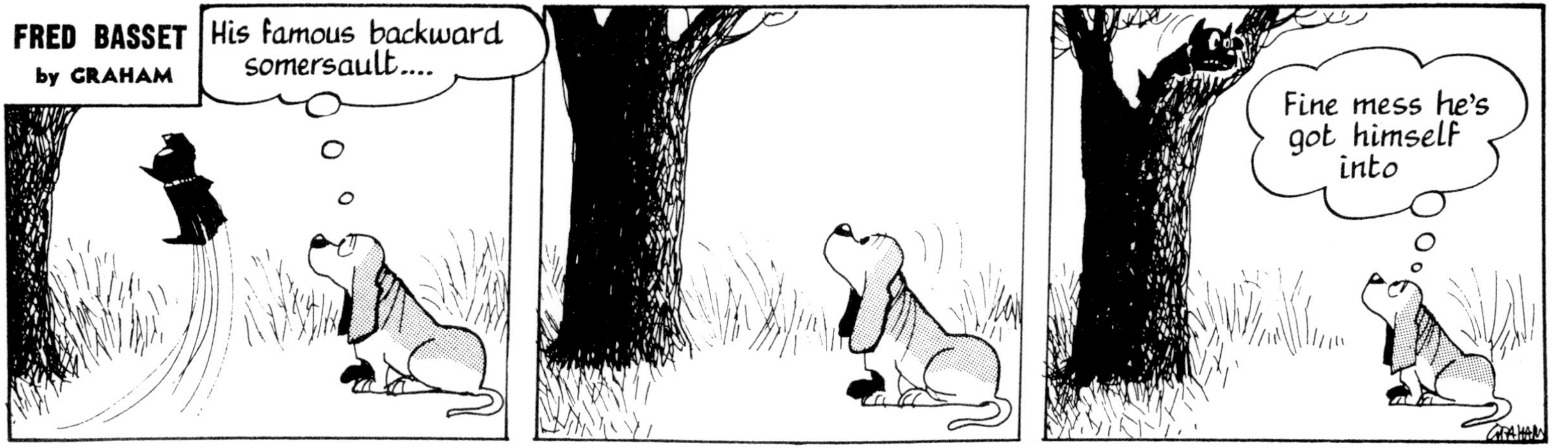
FRED BASSET
by GRAHAM
His famous backward somersault....
Fine mess he's got himself into
GRAHAM

1986

FRED BASSET
by GRAHAM
BEWARE FIERCE DOG
I don't believe in taking risks!
GRAHAM

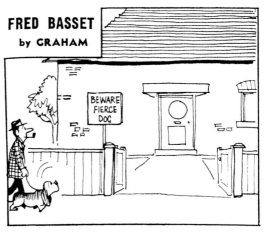

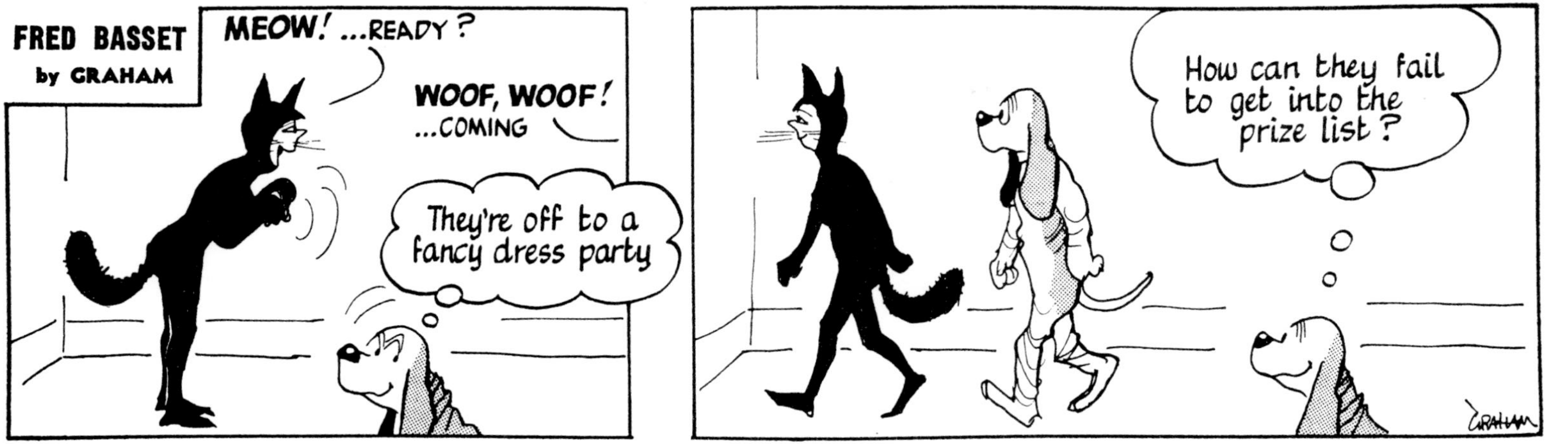
FRED BASSET
by GRAHAM
MEOW! ...READY?
WOOF, WOOF! ...COMING
They're off to a fancy dress party
How can they fail to get into the prize list?
GRAHAM

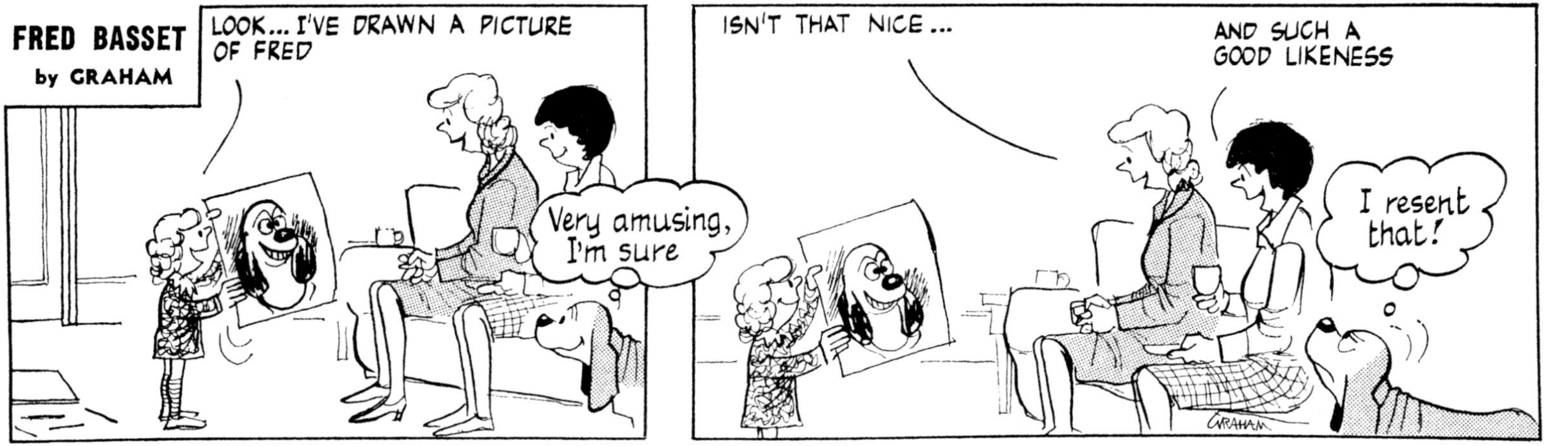
FRED BASSET
by GRAHAM
LOOK... I'VE DRAWN A PICTURE OF FRED
Very amusing, I'm sure
ISN'T THAT NICE...
AND SUCH A GOOD LIKENESS
I resent that!
GRAHAM

1987

FRED BASSET
by GRAHAM

FETCH IT, FRED!

MY WALKING STICK!... WHERE'S MY WALKING STICK?

First things first!

CELEBRATING **50** YEARS

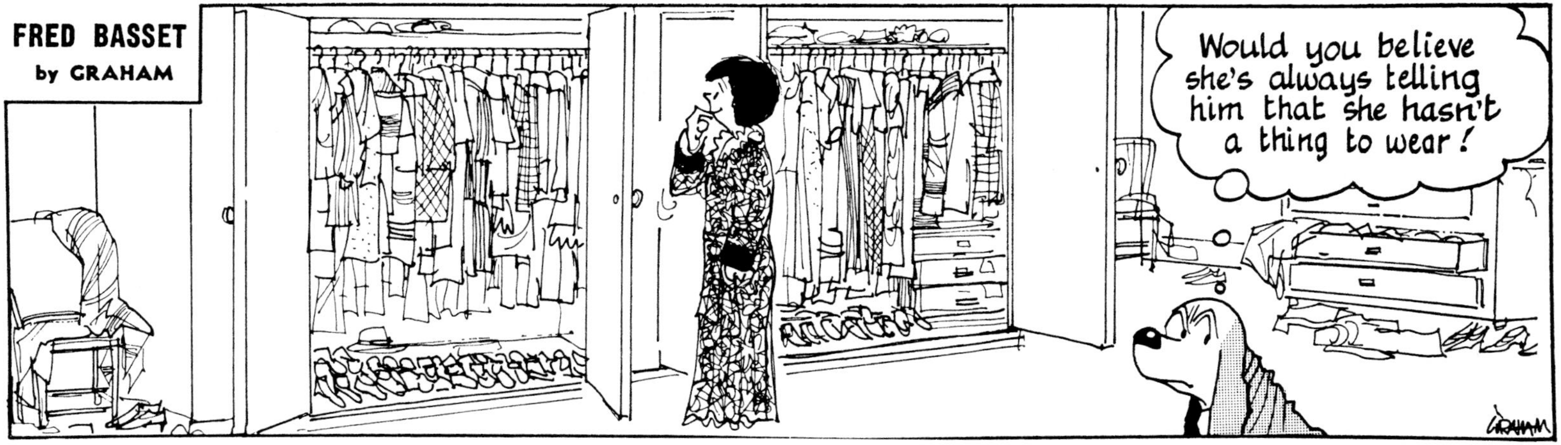
FRED BASSET
by GRAHAM
Would you believe she's always telling him that she hasn't a thing to wear!
GRAHAM

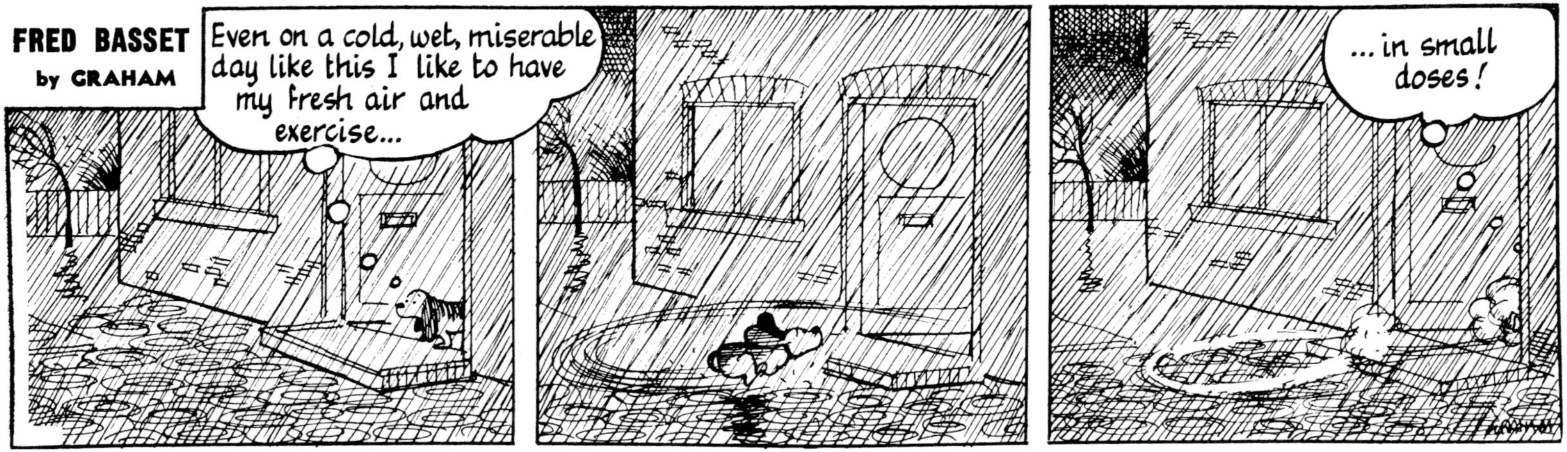
FRED BASSET
by GRAHAM
Even on a cold, wet, miserable day like this I like to have my fresh air and exercise...
... in small doses!

1988

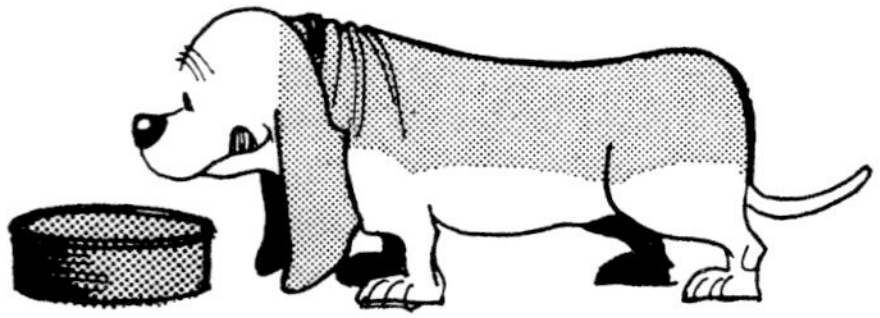

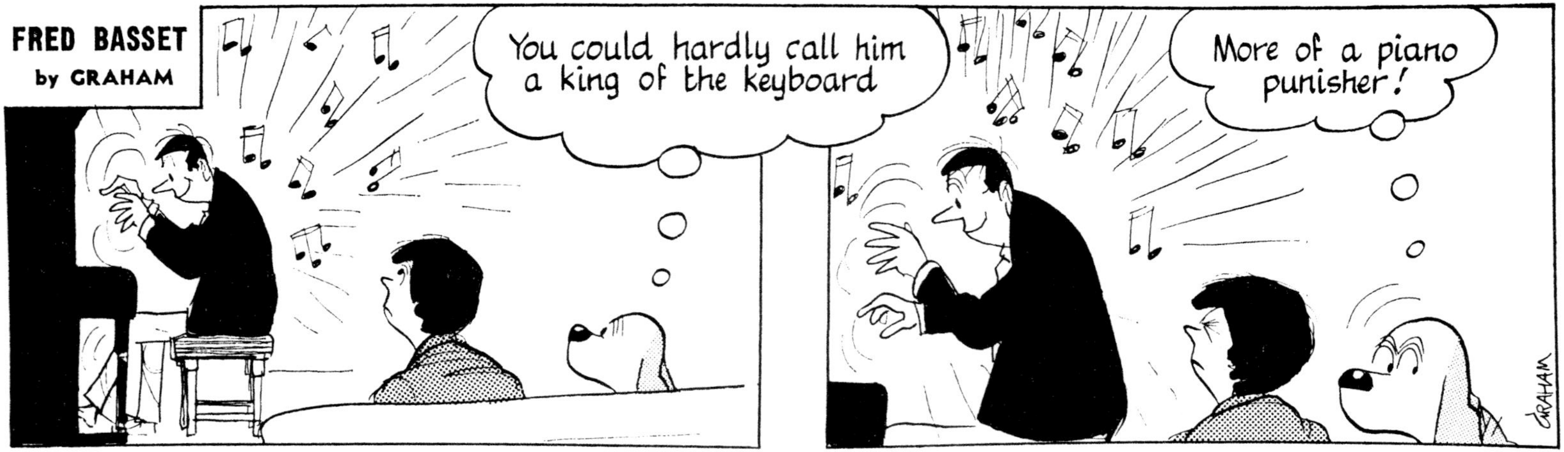
FRED BASSET
by GRAHAM
You could hardly call him a king of the keyboard
More of a piano punisher!
GRAHAM

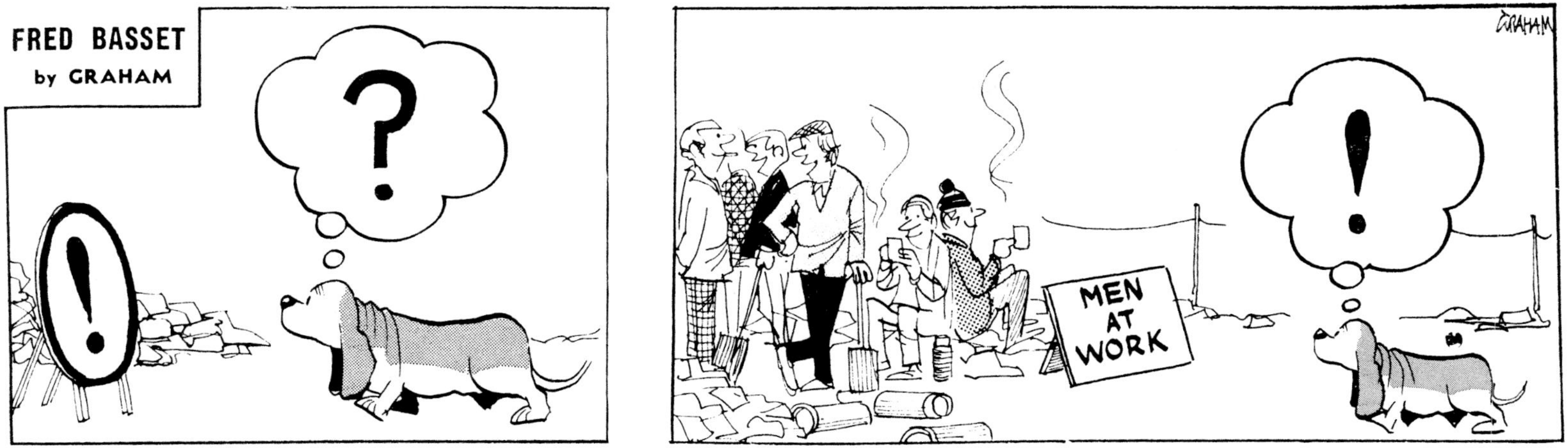
FRED BASSET
by GRAHAM
?
!
GRAHAM
MEN AT WORK
!

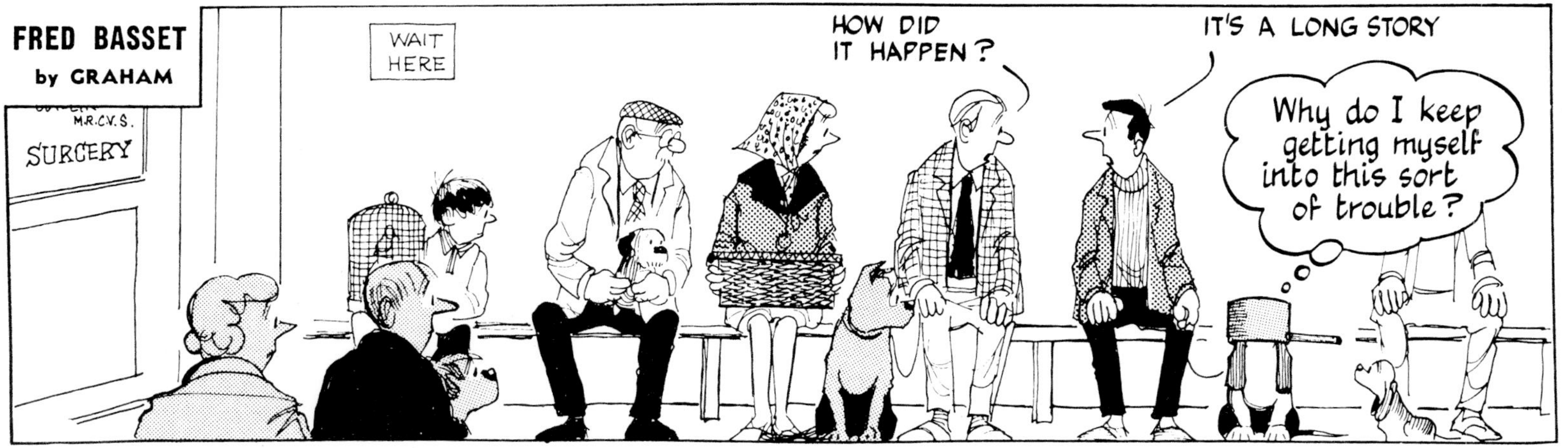
FRED BASSET
by GRAHAM
WAIT HERE
M.R.C.V.S.
SURGERY
HOW DID IT HAPPEN?
IT'S A LONG STORY
Why do I keep getting myself into this sort of trouble?

1989

What a night to go out for a walk!
A barrel of brandy round my neck, and we could be a mountain rescue team

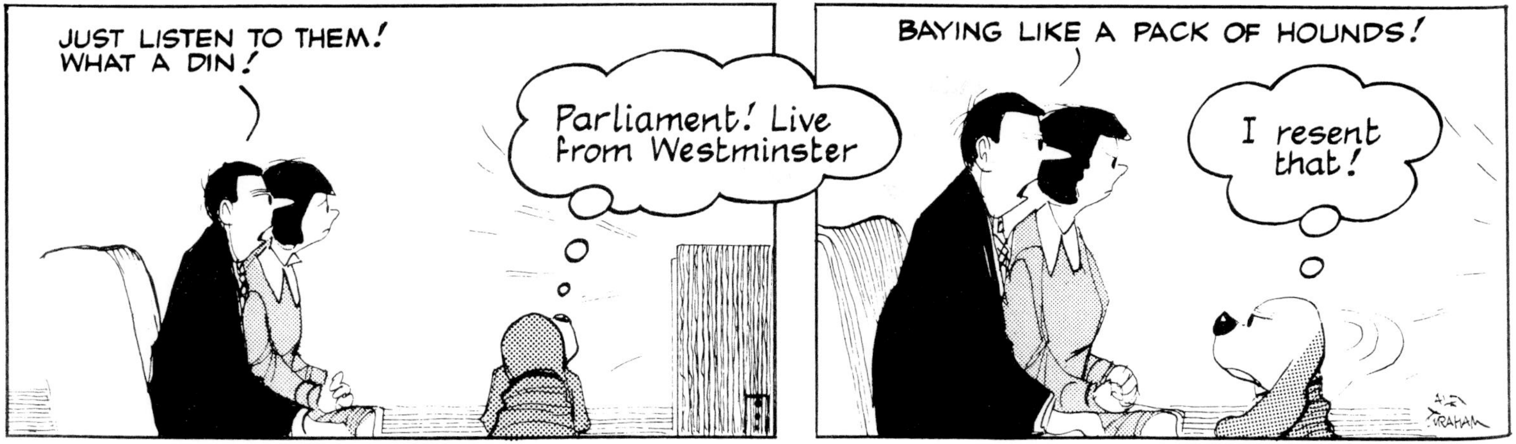
JUST LISTEN TO THEM! WHAT A DIN!
Parliament! Live from Westminster
BAYING LIKE A PACK OF HOUNDS!
I resent that!

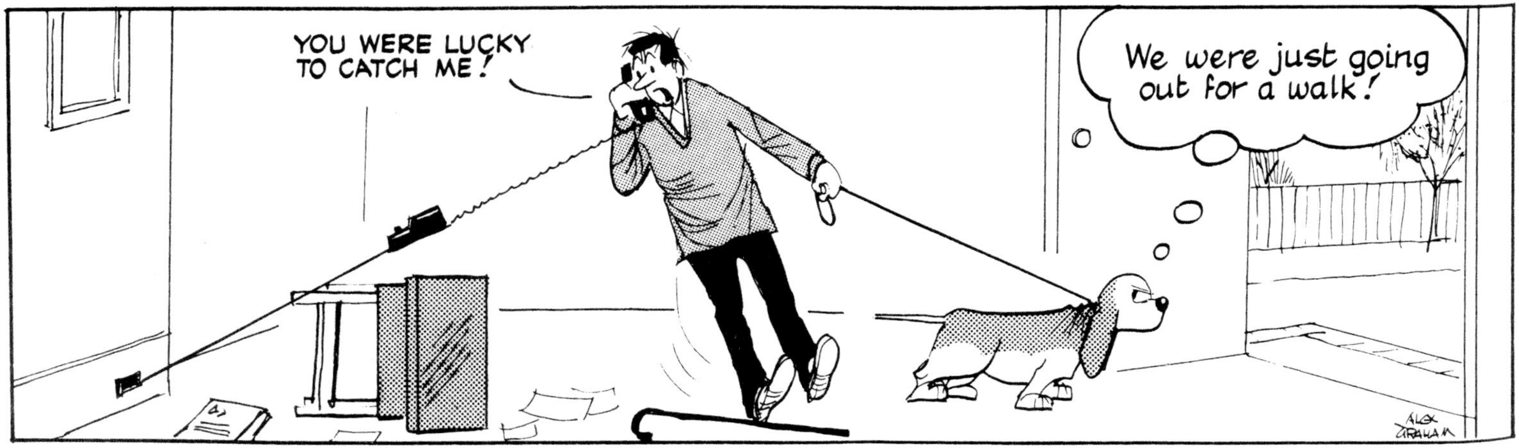
YOU WERE LUCKY TO CATCH ME!
We were just going out for a walk!

1990

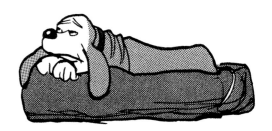

THIS IS A LOVELY BEAUNE

For me ?

IN PERFECT CONDITION

Where is this lovely bone ?

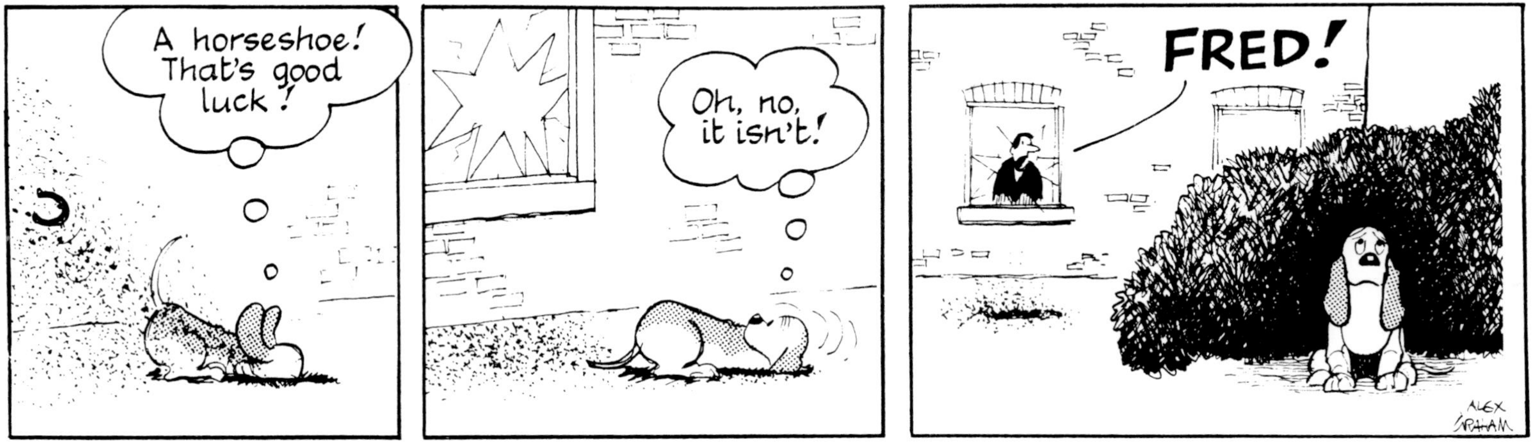
A horseshoe! That's good luck!
Oh, no, it isn't!
FRED!
ALEX GRAHAM

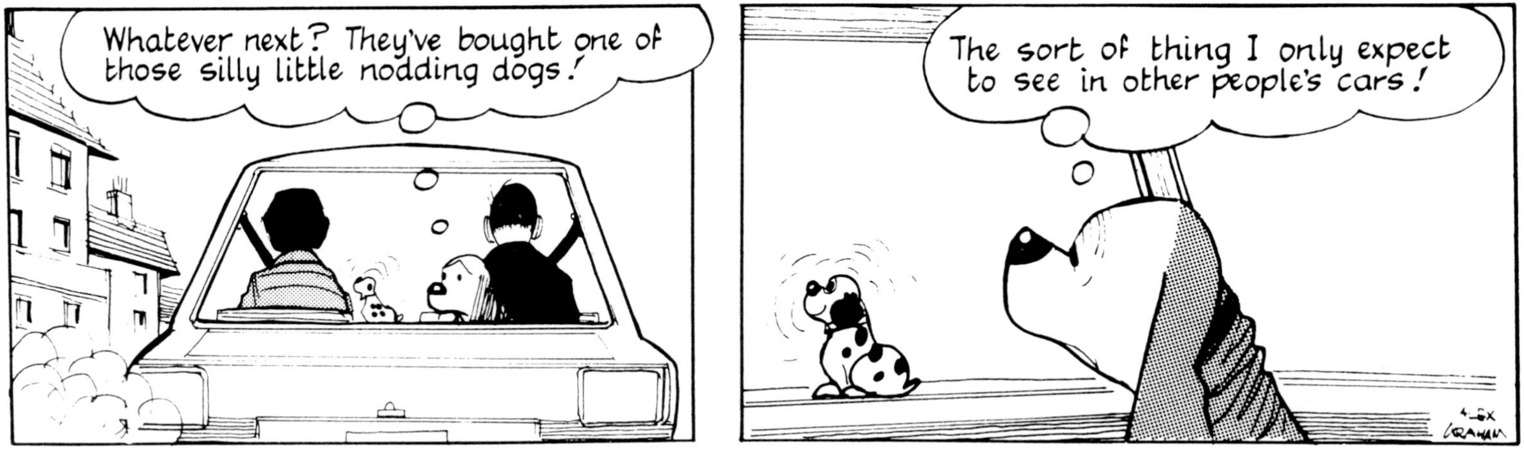
Whatever next? They've bought one of those silly little nodding dogs!
The sort of thing I only expect to see in other people's cars!
ALEX GRAHAM

1991

REMEMBER THIS? FRED IN THE FANCY DRESS DOG SHOW AT THE CHURCH FÊTE
I was a disappointing second
Pipped by Jock in a wee kilt and Glengarry bonnet
ALEX GRAHAM

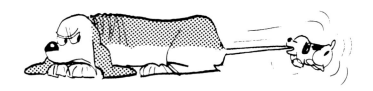

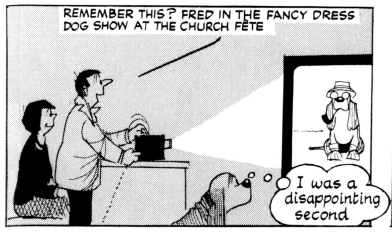

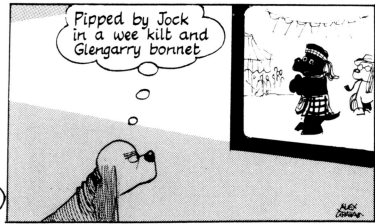

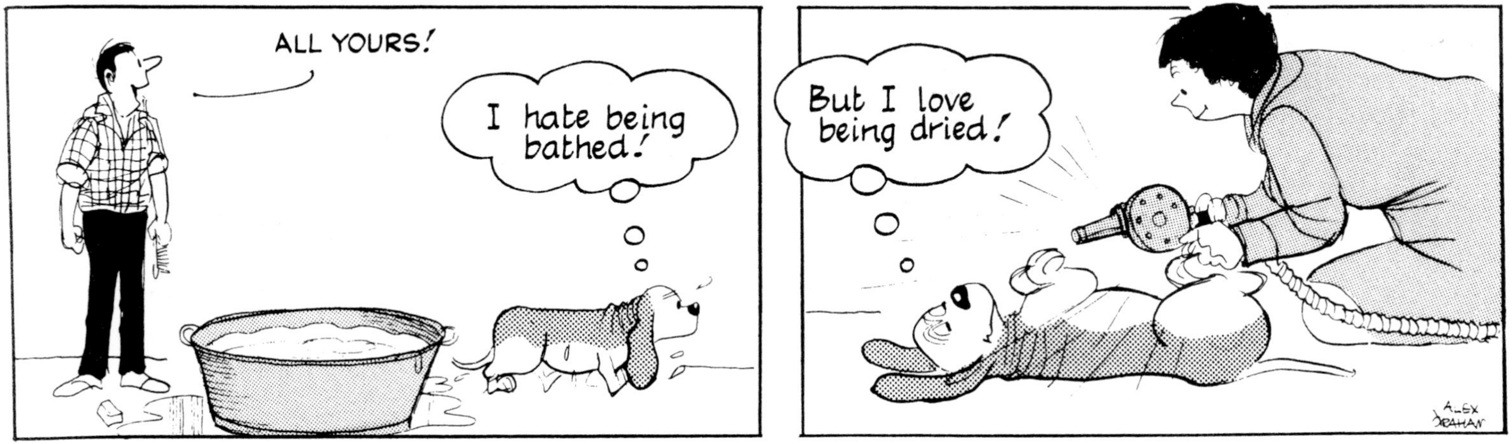
ALL YOURS!
I hate being bathed!
But I love being dried!

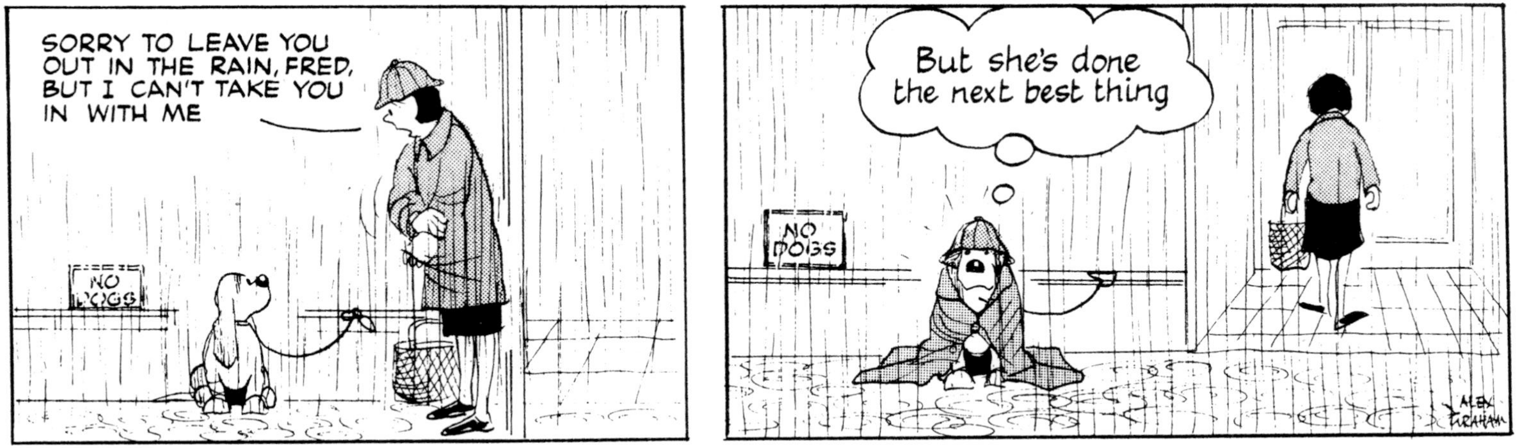
SORRY TO LEAVE YOU OUT IN THE RAIN, FRED, BUT I CAN'T TAKE YOU IN WITH ME
NO DOGS
But she's done the next best thing
NO DOGS

1992

That takes me back to my puppy days
My old toy cupboard
ALEX GRAHAM

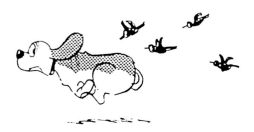

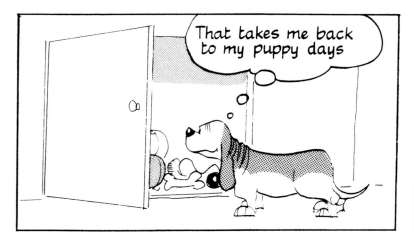

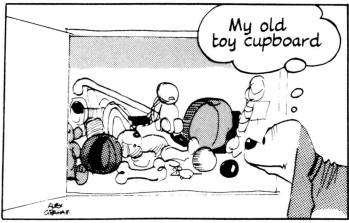

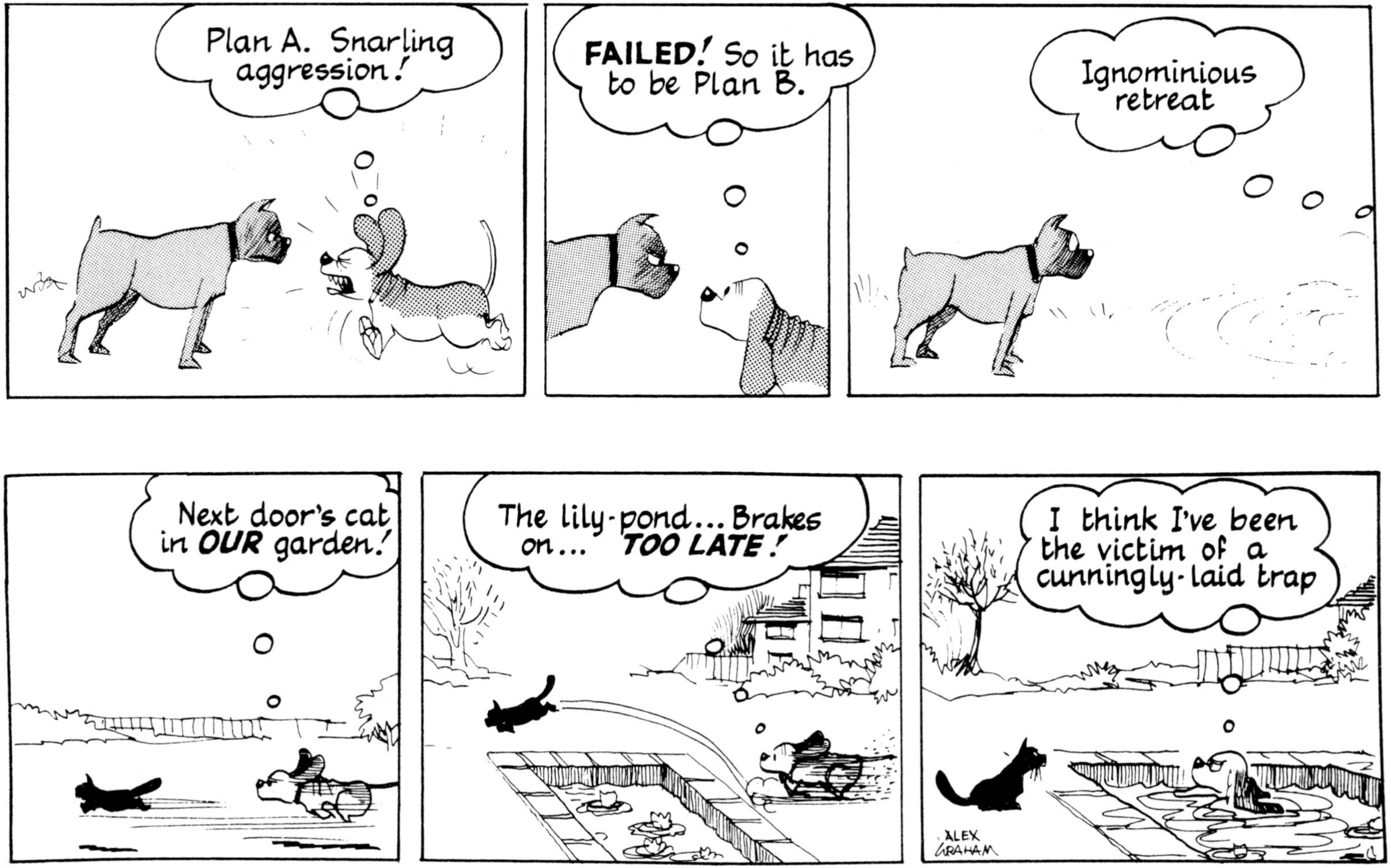
Plan A. Snarling aggression!
FAILED! So it has to be Plan B.
Ignominious retreat
Next door's cat in OUR garden!
The lily-pond... Brakes on... TOO LATE!
I think I've been the victim of a cunningly-laid trap
ALEX GRAHAM

1993

UNMATCHED FOR FLAVOUR
AND QUALITY...
AMBER CLEAR...
SMOOTH... SATISFYING...
THE PERFECT PINT—
SNOOKS' BITTER
The power of advertising
JUST TAKING FRED FOR A WALK
They have it on draught at our local!
ALEX GRAHAM

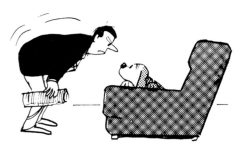

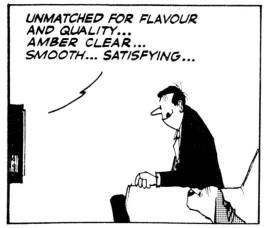

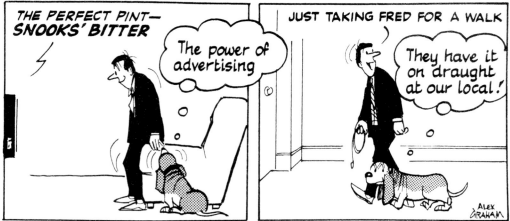

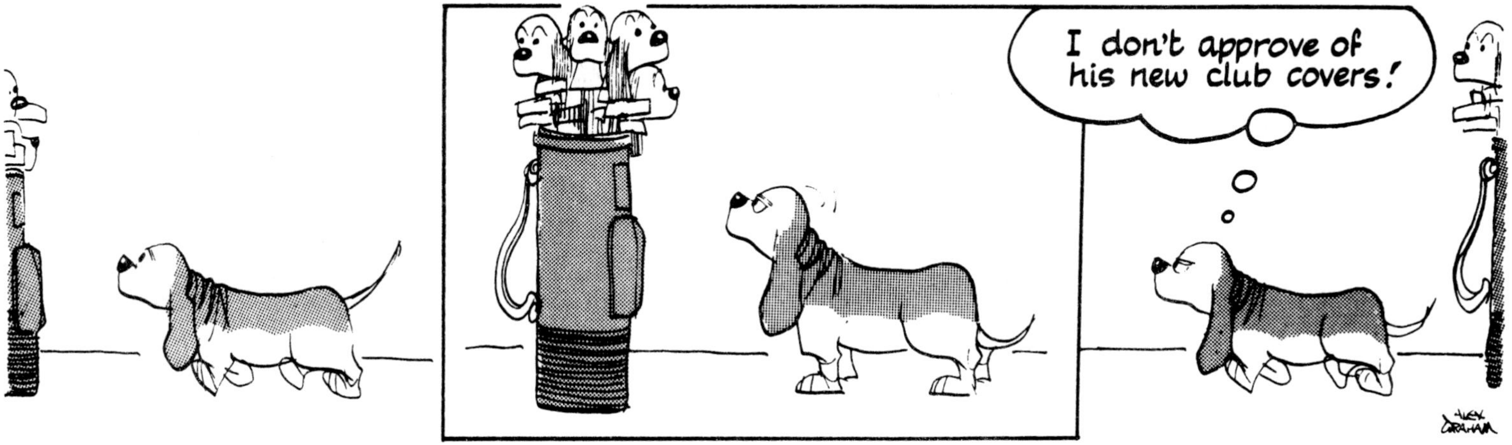
I don't approve of his new club covers!
ALEX GRAHAM

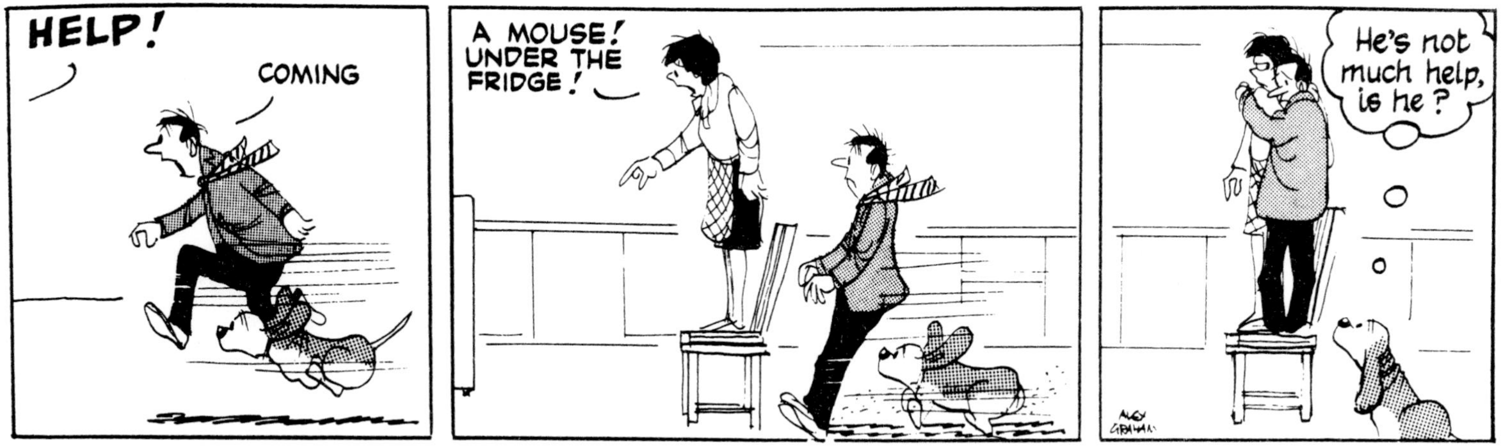
HELP!
COMING
A MOUSE! UNDER THE FRIDGE!
ALEX GRAHAM
He's not much help, is he?

1994

BANG! BANG!
GOT YOU!
WOOF! WOOF!
Got you back

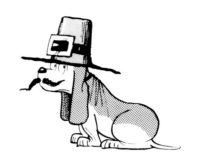

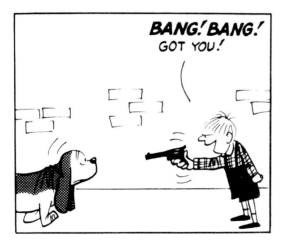

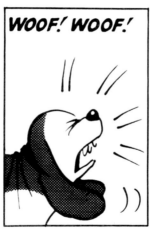

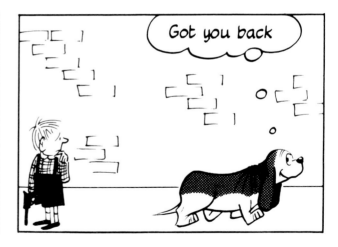

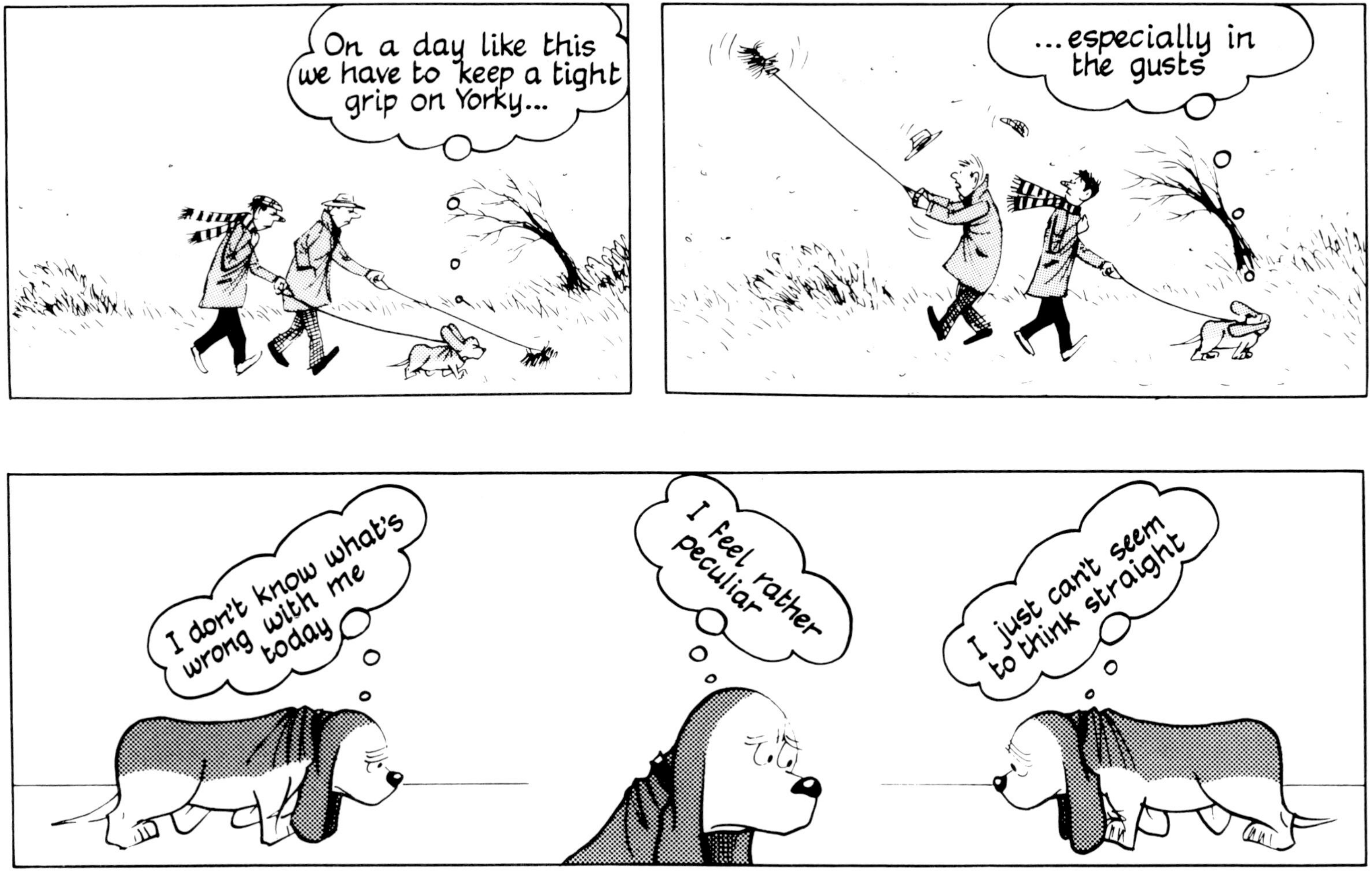
On a day like this we have to keep a tight grip on Yorky...
...especially in the gusts
I don't know what's wrong with me today
I feel rather peculiar
I just can't seem to think straight

1995

...AND THIS WEEK'S WINNING NUMBERS IN THE NATIONAL LOTTERY ARE...
They have all these fantastic plans if they win. A large house in the country, exotic holidays, fancy cars...
A lifetime's supply of Doggybix would suit **me**!

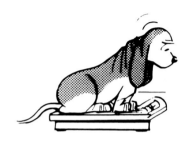

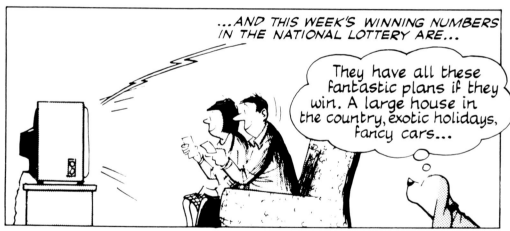

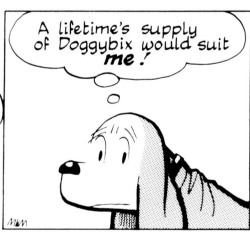

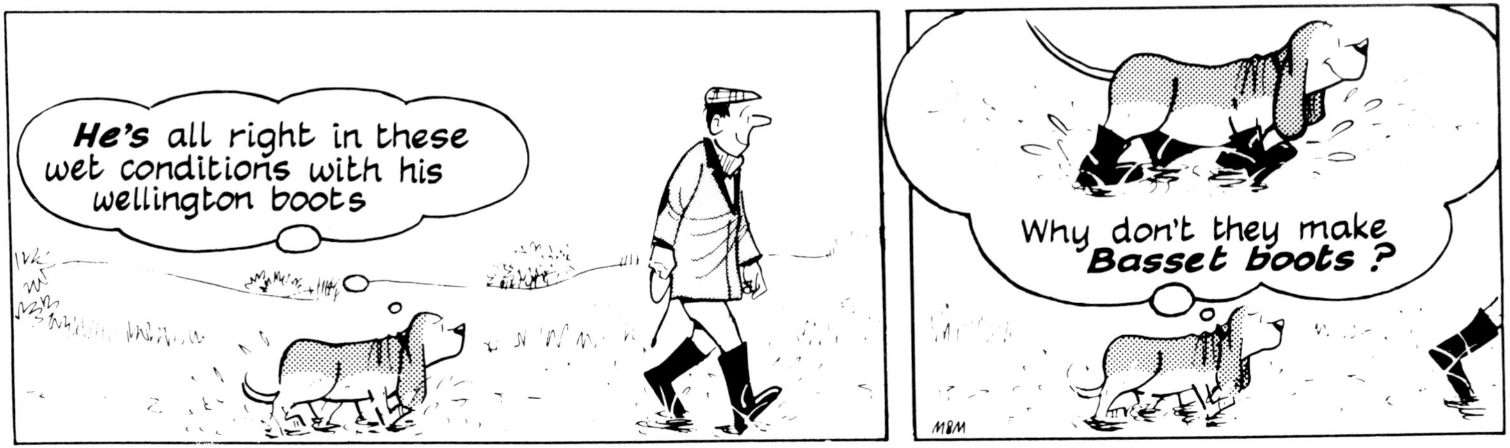
He's all right in these wet conditions with his wellington boots
Why don't they make *Basset boots* ?

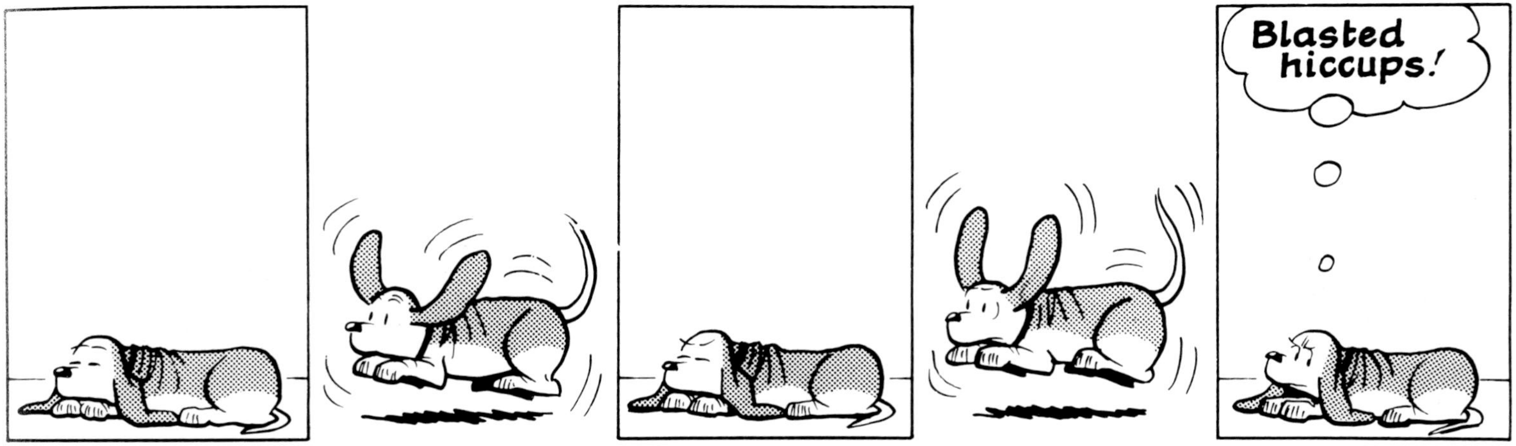
Blasted hiccups!

1996

Good gracious! I didn't realise I'd been asleep that long!

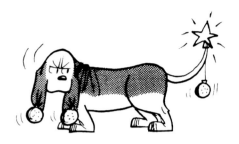

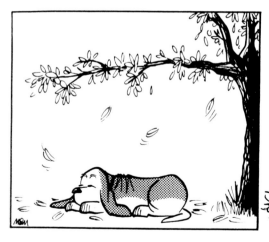

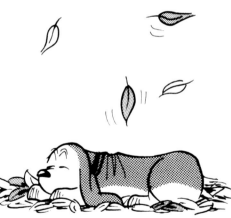

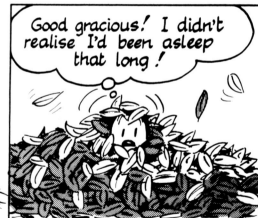

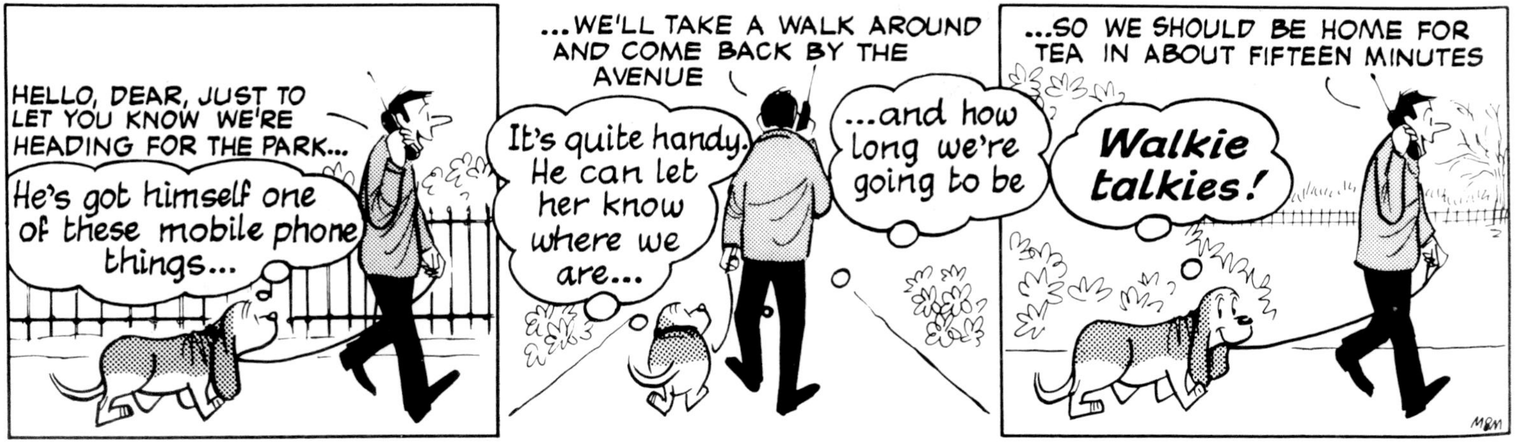
HELLO, DEAR, JUST TO LET YOU KNOW WE'RE HEADING FOR THE PARK...
He's got himself one of these mobile phone things...
...WE'LL TAKE A WALK AROUND AND COME BACK BY THE AVENUE
It's quite handy. He can let her know where we are...
...and how long we're going to be
...SO WE SHOULD BE HOME FOR TEA IN ABOUT FIFTEEN MINUTES
Walkie talkies!

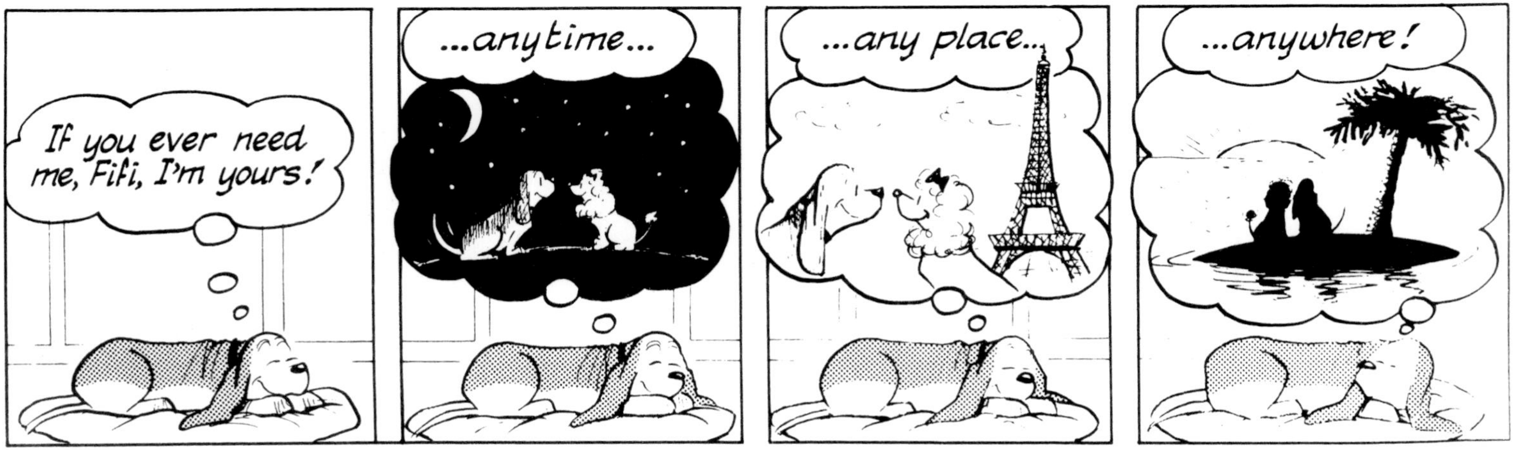
If you ever need me, Fifi, I'm yours!
...anytime...
...any place...
...anywhere!

1997

Her friend Angela has brought round little Tommy...
...let's see what he's up to
Well, well! Who's a clever boy, then?
FRED

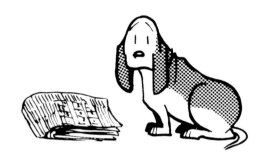

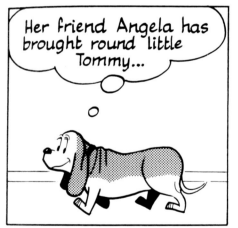

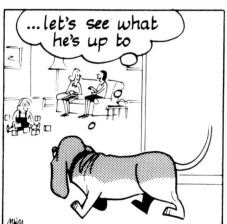

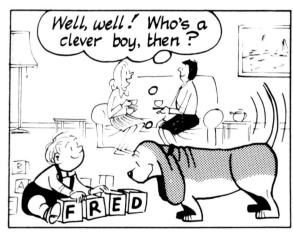

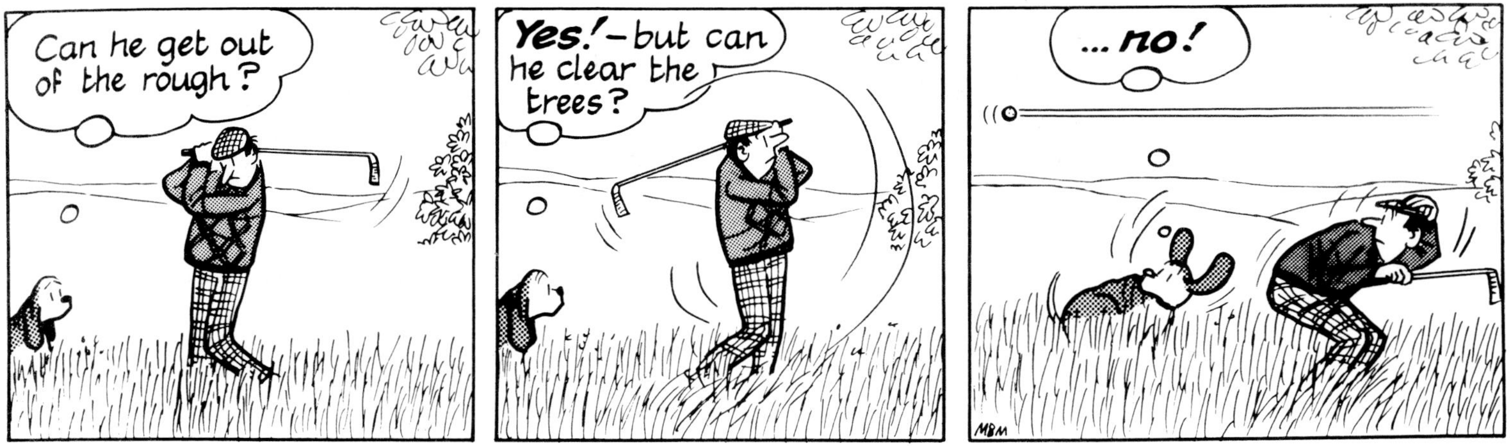
Can he get out of the rough?
Yes! – but can he clear the trees?
... no!
MBM

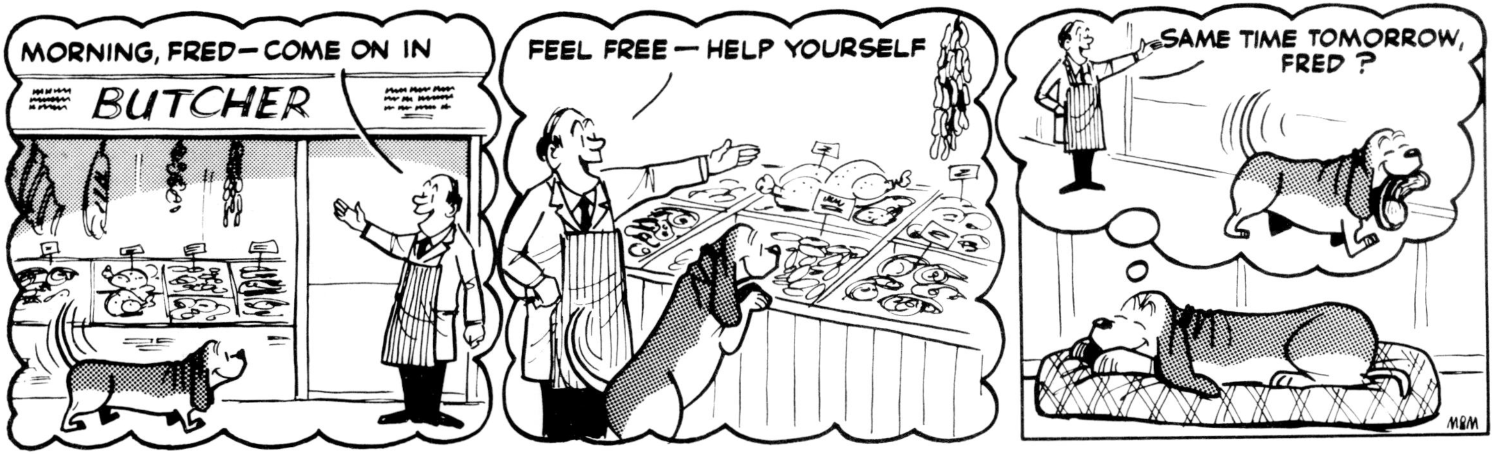
MORNING, FRED – COME ON IN
BUTCHER
FEEL FREE – HELP YOURSELF
SAME TIME TOMORROW, FRED?
MBM

1998

WHAT'S FRED BARKING AT ?
I'M NOT SURE
... IT'S EITHER ROLF HARRIS OR THE FLUFFY RABBIT HE'S HOLDING

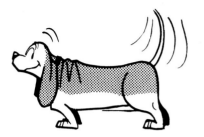

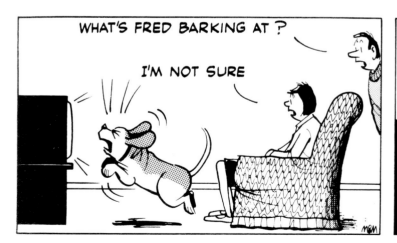

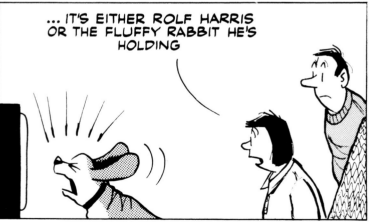

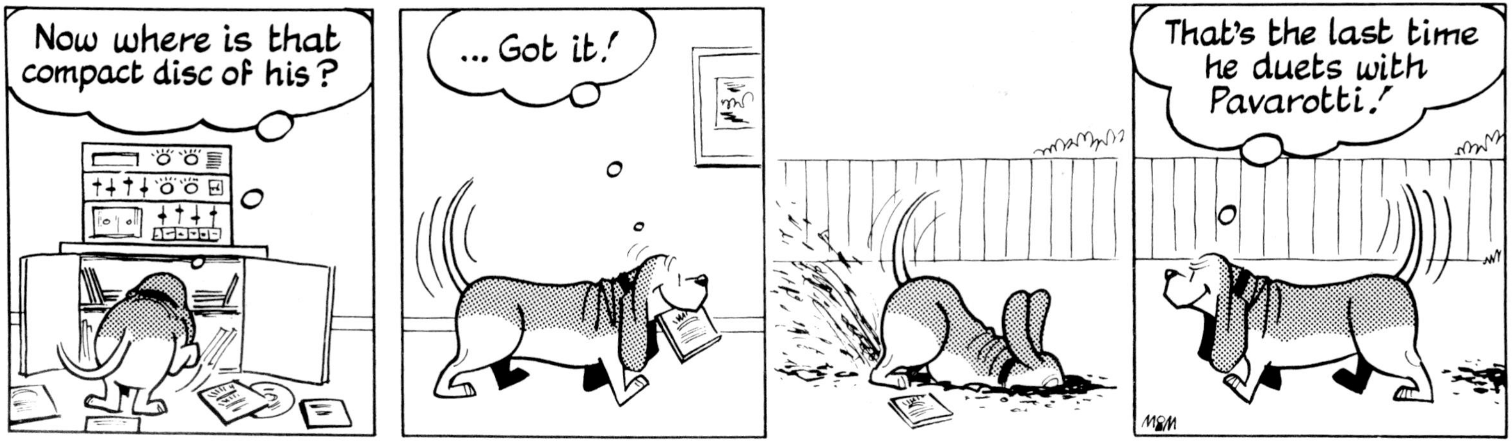
Now where is that compact disc of his?
... Got it!
That's the last time he duets with Pavarotti!
M&M

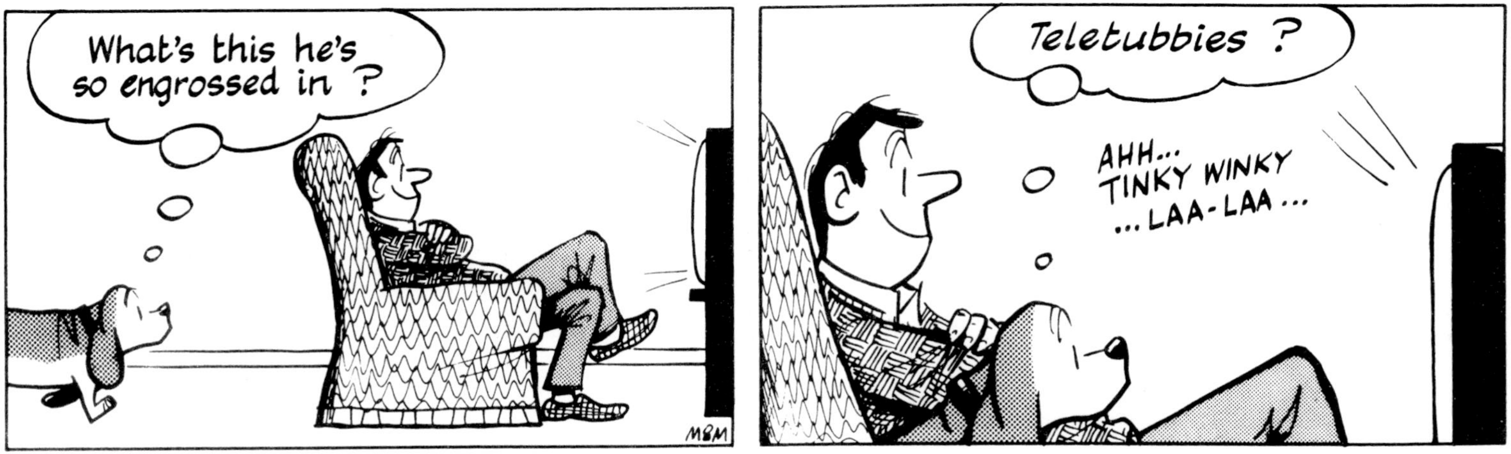
What's this he's so engrossed in ?
M&M
Teletubbies ?
AHH... TINKY WINKY ... LAA-LAA ...

1999

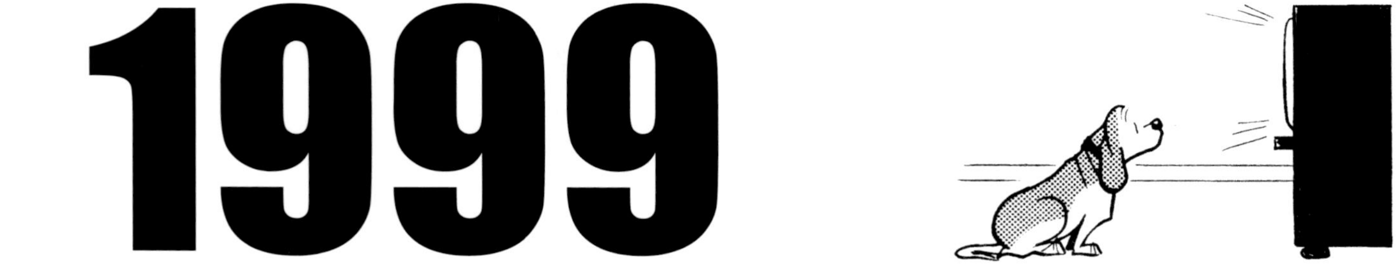

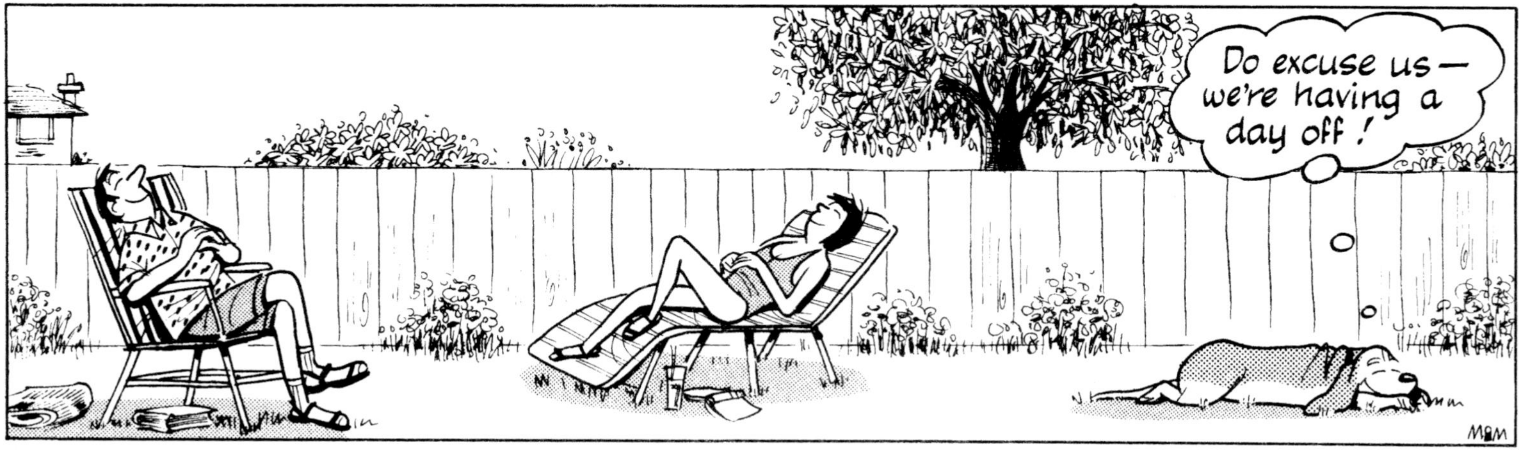
Do excuse us— we're having a day off!
MGM

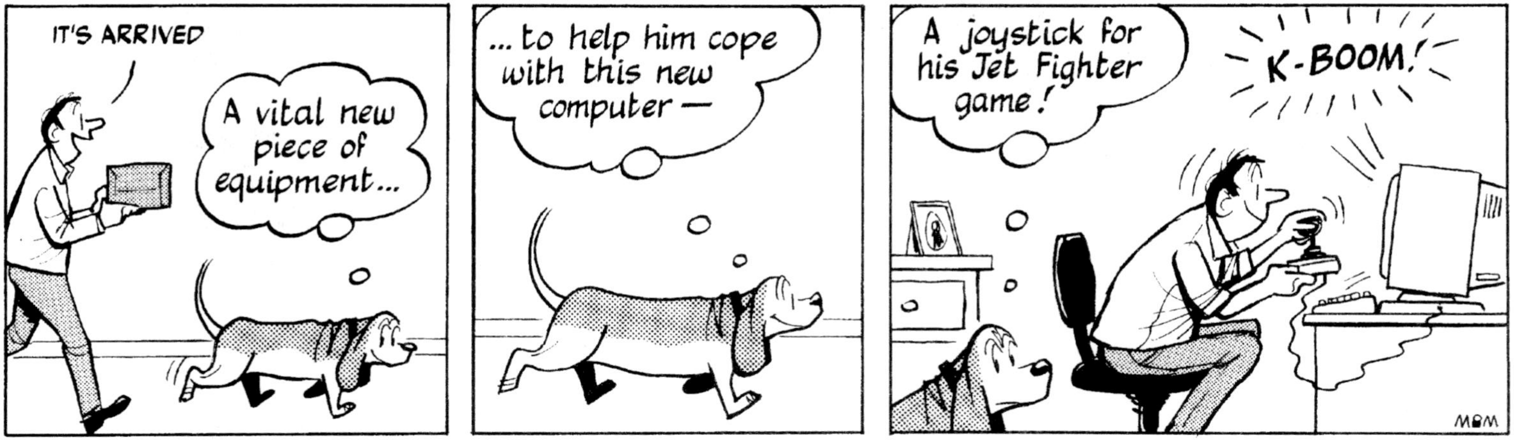
IT'S ARRIVED
A vital new piece of equipment...
...to help him cope with this new computer —
A joystick for his Jet Fighter game!
K-BOOM!

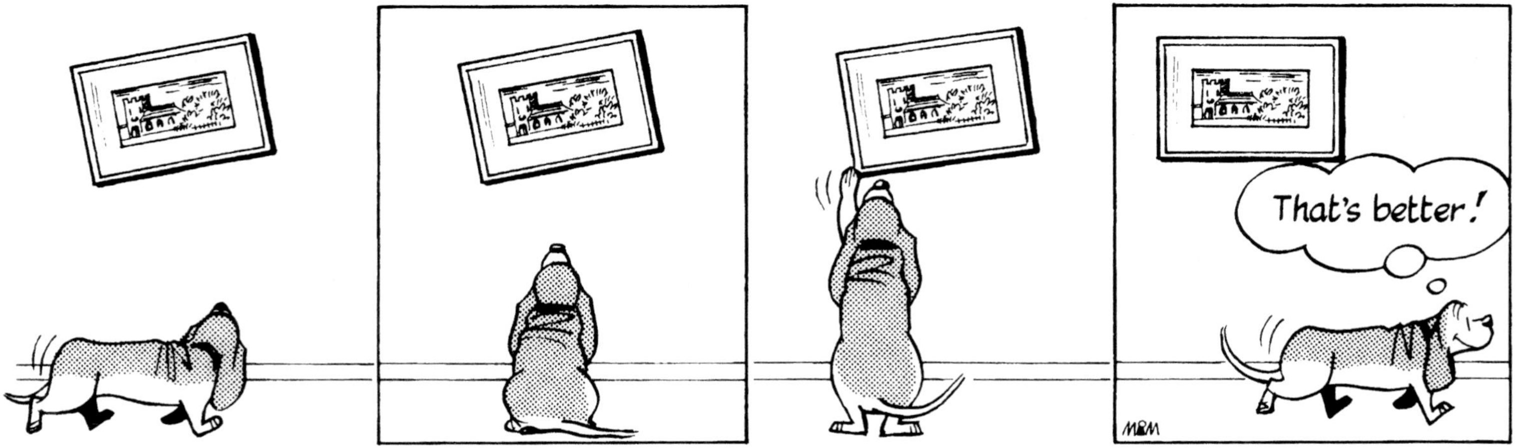
That's better!

2000

NUITS ST. GEORGES '85
MGM
Shame. It was a good year!

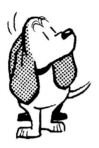

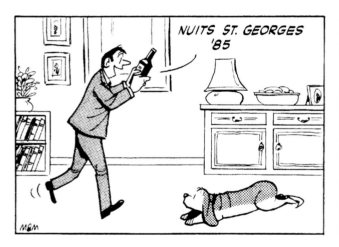

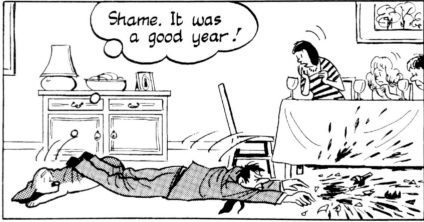

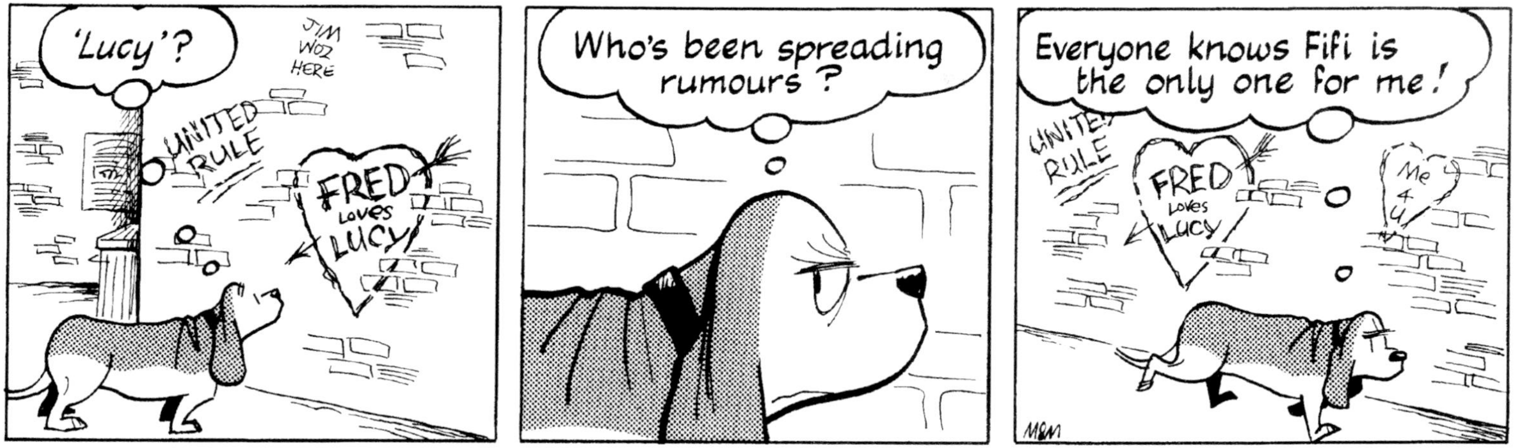
'Lucy'?
JIM WOZ HERE
UNITED RULE
FRED loves LUCY
Who's been spreading rumours ?
Everyone knows Fifi is the only one for me!
UNITED RULE
FRED loves LUCY
Me 4 U

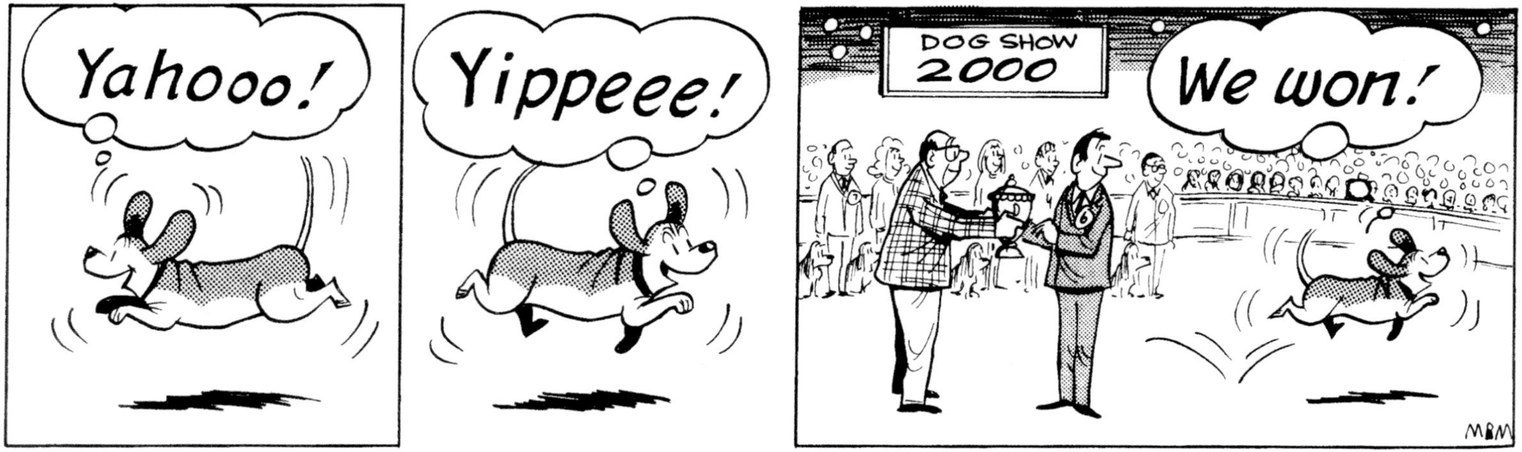
Yahooo!
Yippeee!
DOG SHOW 2000
We won!

2001

SHOO!
Fat lot of good you are!
MGM

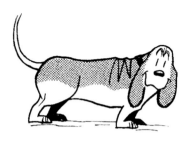

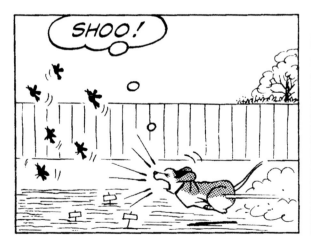

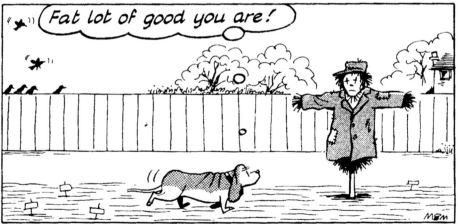

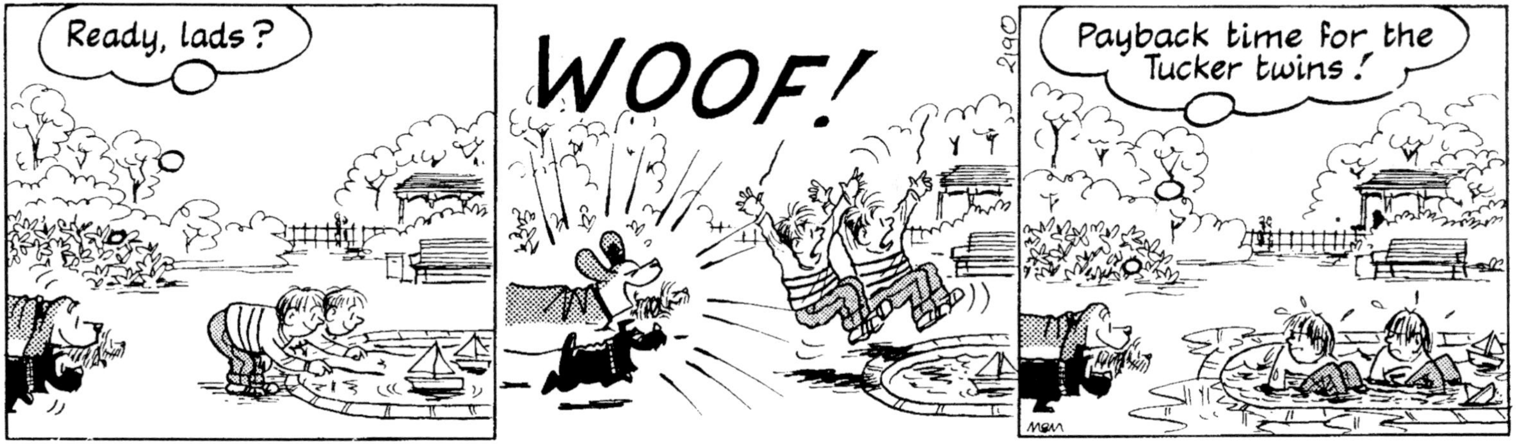
Ready, lads?
WOOF!
2190
Payback time for the Tucker twins!
MGM

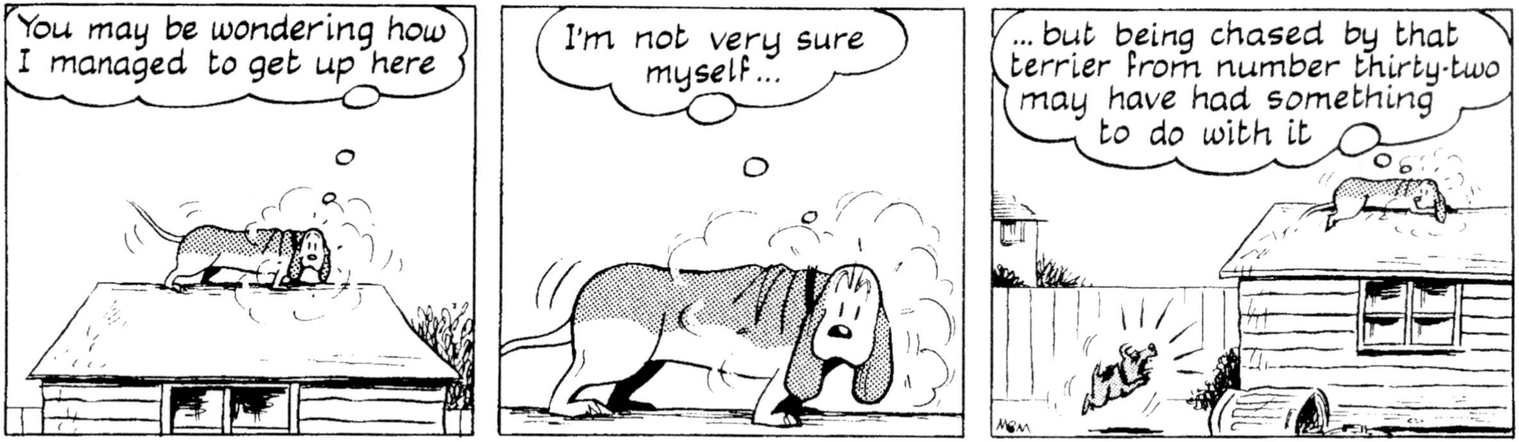
You may be wondering how I managed to get up here
I'm not very sure myself...
... but being chased by that terrier from number thirty-two may have had something to do with it
MGM

2002

GRRRRRRRR!
MGM
That was impressive, wasn't it ?

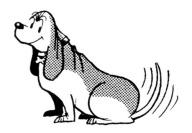

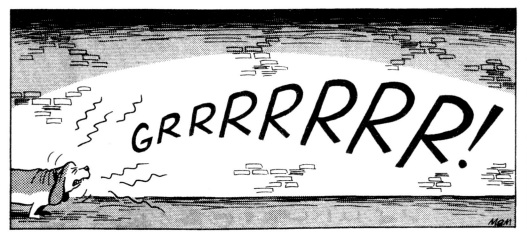

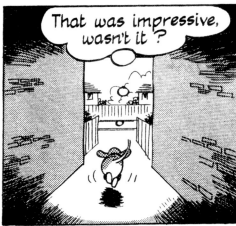

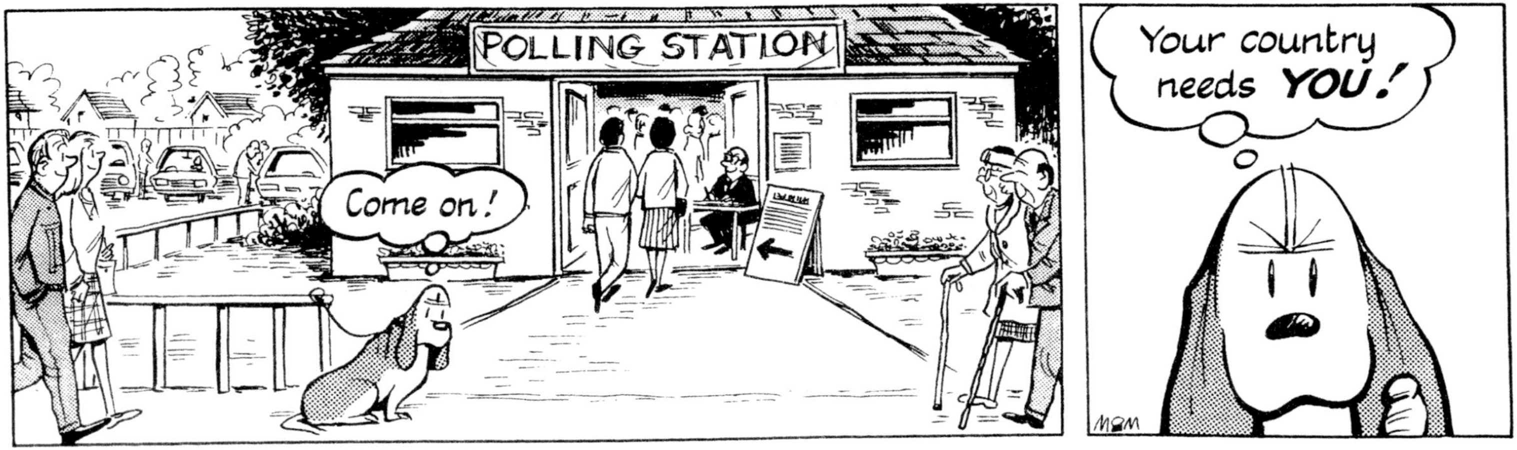
POLLING STATION
Come on!
Your country needs YOU!

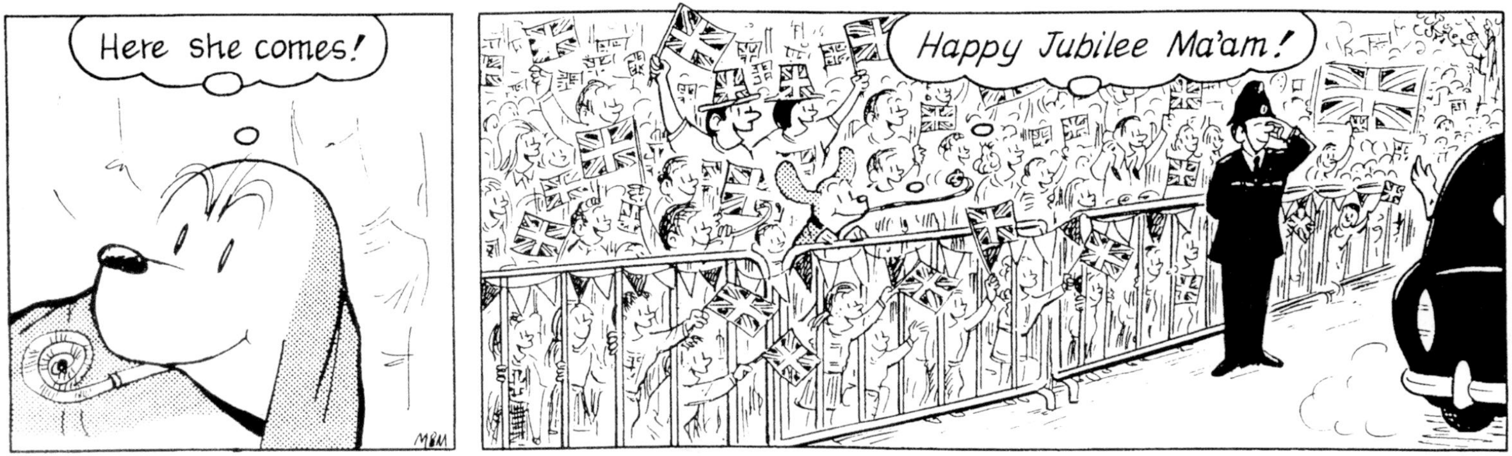
Here she comes!
Happy Jubilee Ma'am!

2003

QUICK, PASS ME THE CAMERA!
MGM
22
16
11
8
5·6
4
2·8
1·8

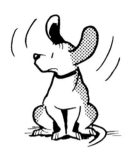

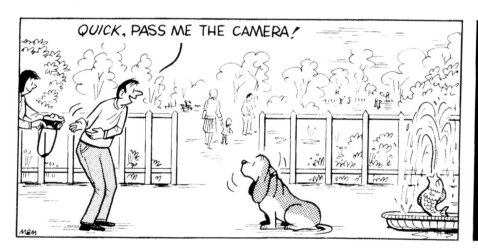

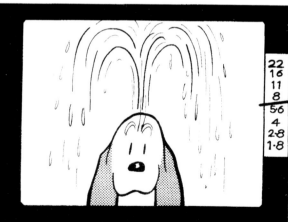

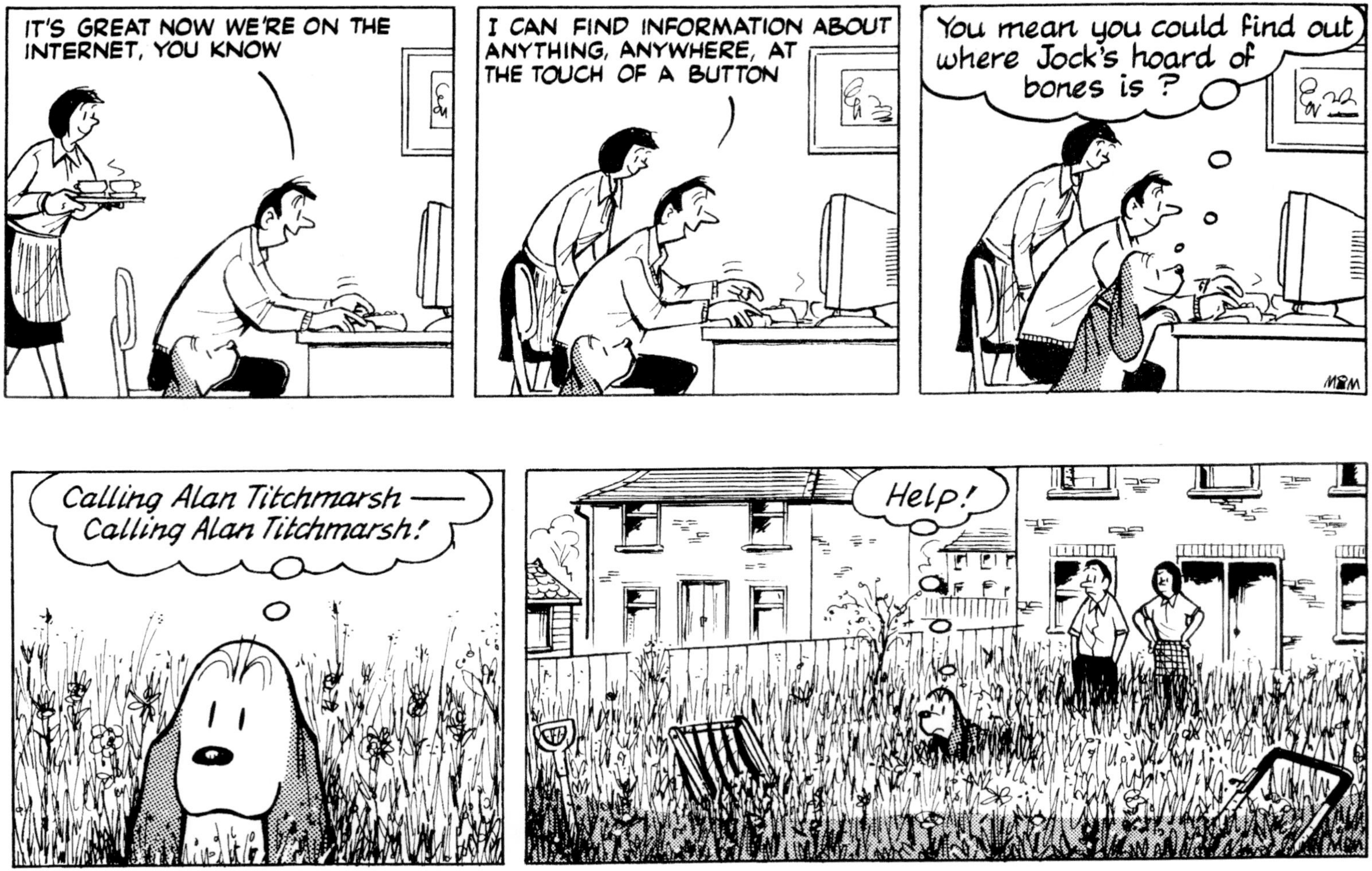
IT'S GREAT NOW WE'RE ON THE INTERNET, YOU KNOW
I CAN FIND INFORMATION ABOUT ANYTHING, ANYWHERE, AT THE TOUCH OF A BUTTON
You mean you could find out where Jock's hoard of bones is ?
Calling Alan Titchmarsh — Calling Alan Titchmarsh!
Help!

2004

Blimey, Jock! News travels fast around here!
We've been rumbled already!
DARING RAID
FULL REPORT

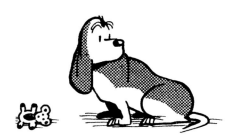

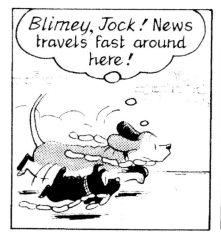

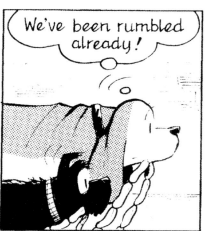

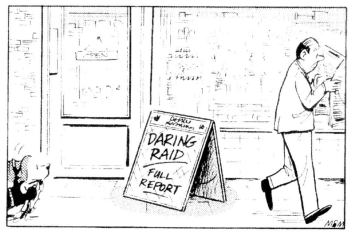

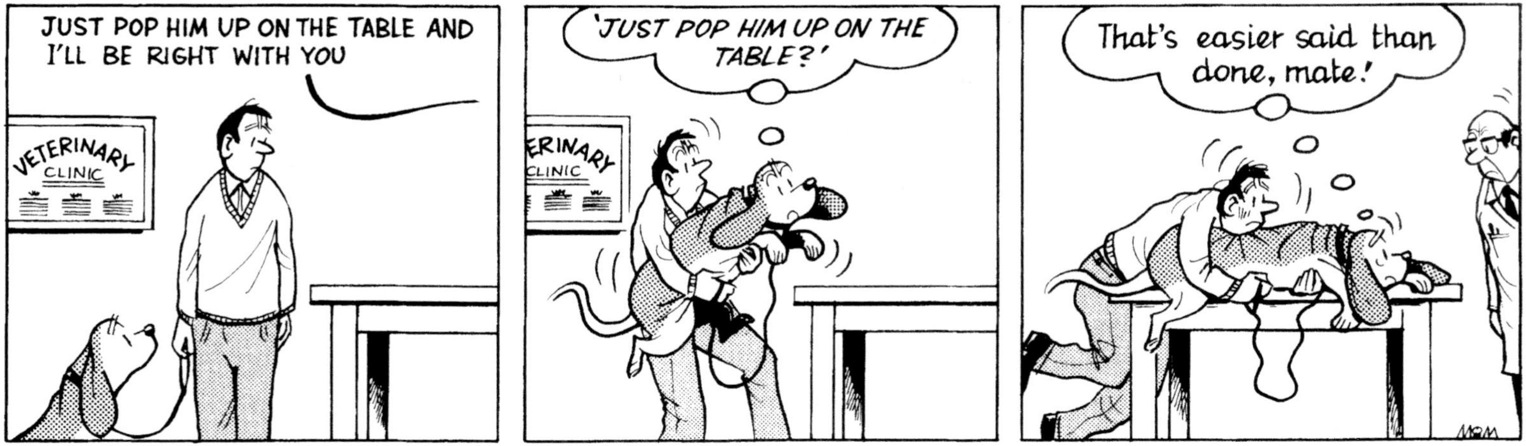
JUST POP HIM UP ON THE TABLE AND I'LL BE RIGHT WITH YOU
VETERINARY CLINIC
'JUST POP HIM UP ON THE TABLE?'
That's easier said than done, mate!

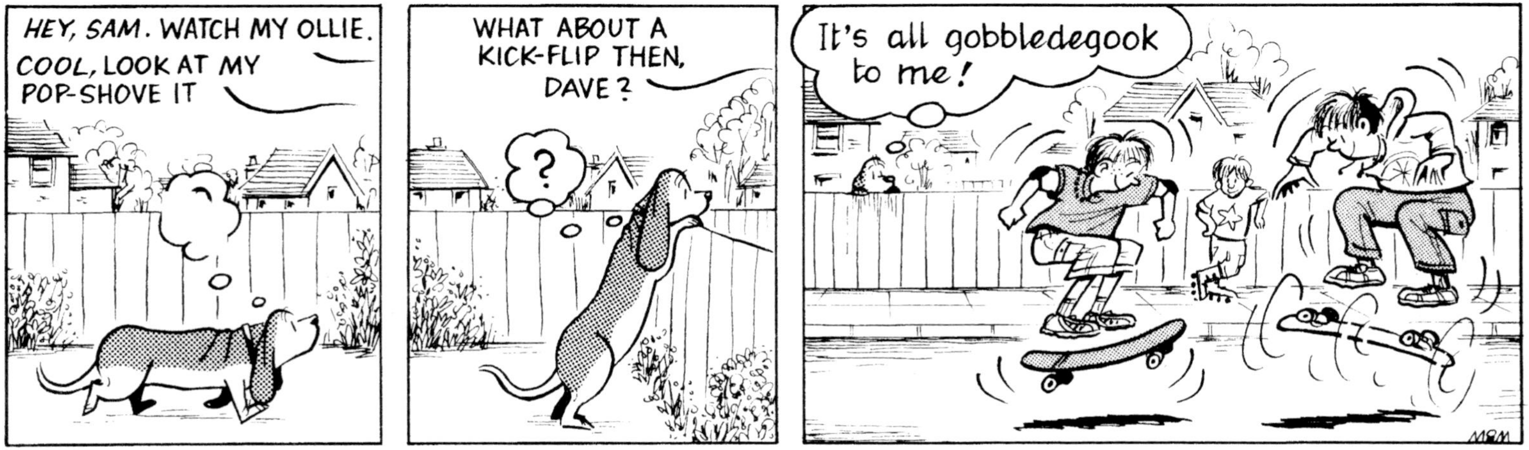
HEY, SAM. WATCH MY OLLIE.
COOL, LOOK AT MY POP-SHOVE IT
WHAT ABOUT A KICK-FLIP THEN, DAVE?
?
It's all gobbledegook to me!

2005

Yorky's taken the lead in the Boat Race...
...but Jock's gaining fast!
McM

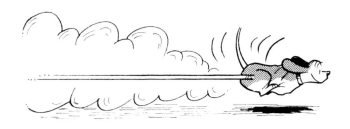

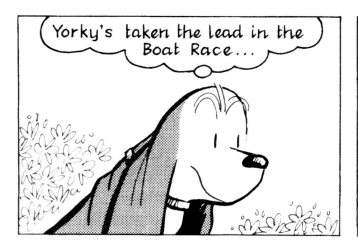

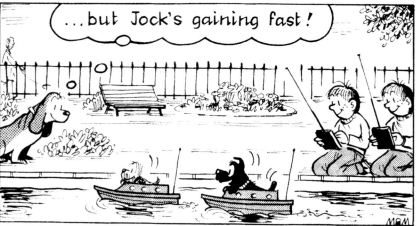

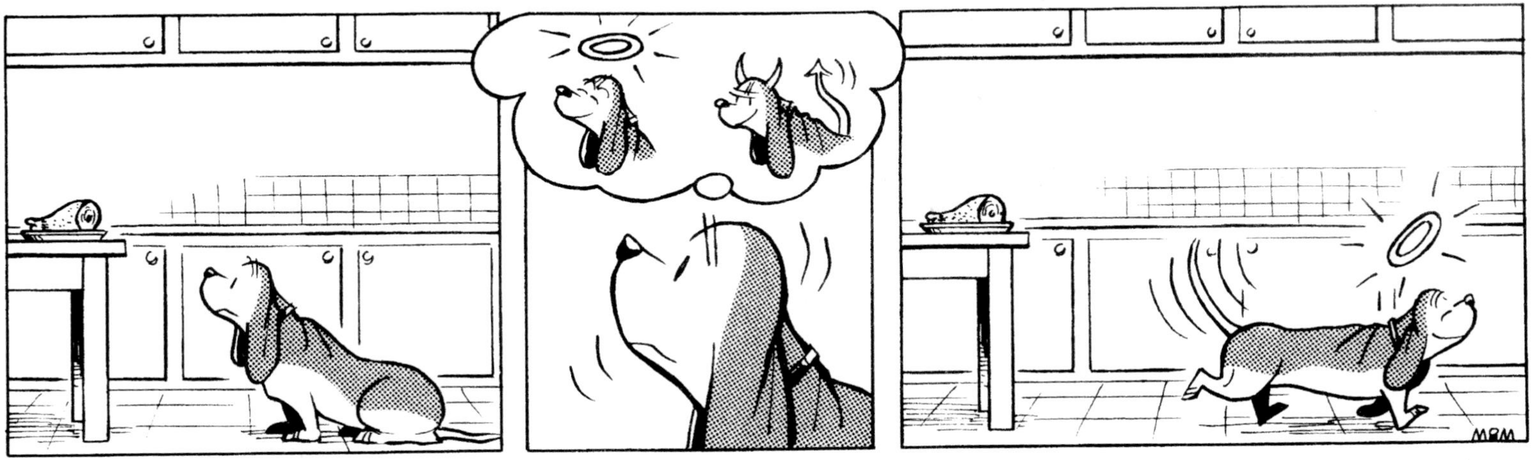

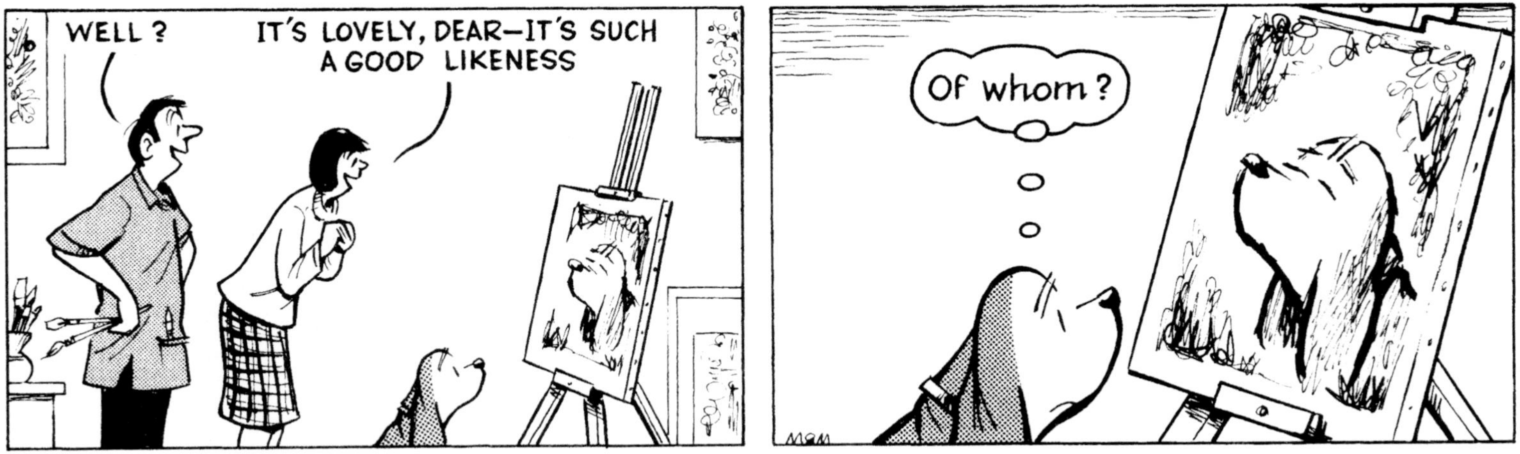
WELL ?
IT'S LOVELY, DEAR—IT'S SUCH A GOOD LIKENESS
Of whom ?

2006

GIANT
BOOT
FAIR

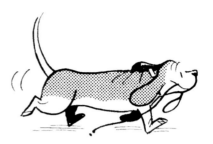

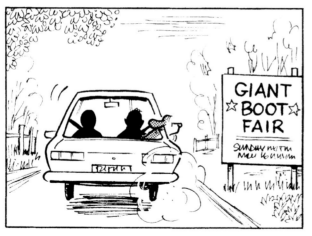

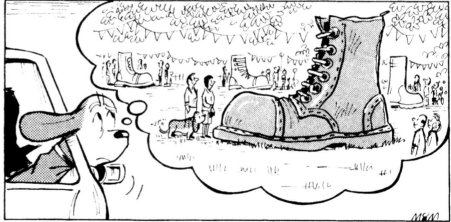

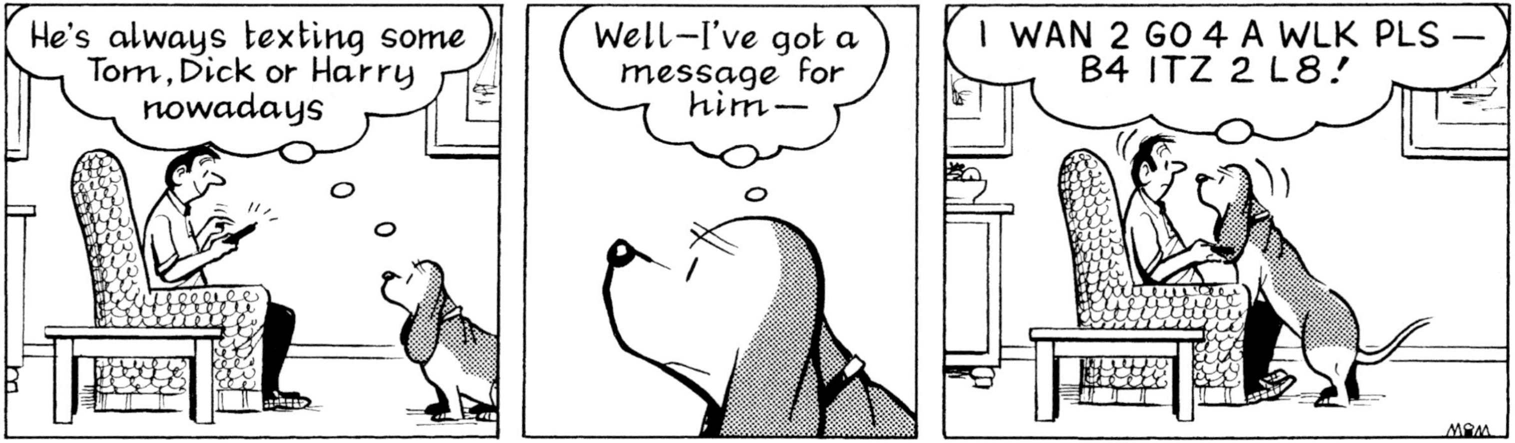
He's always texting some Tom, Dick or Harry nowadays
Well—I've got a message for him—
I WAN 2 GO 4 A WLK PLS — B4 ITZ 2 L8!
MGM

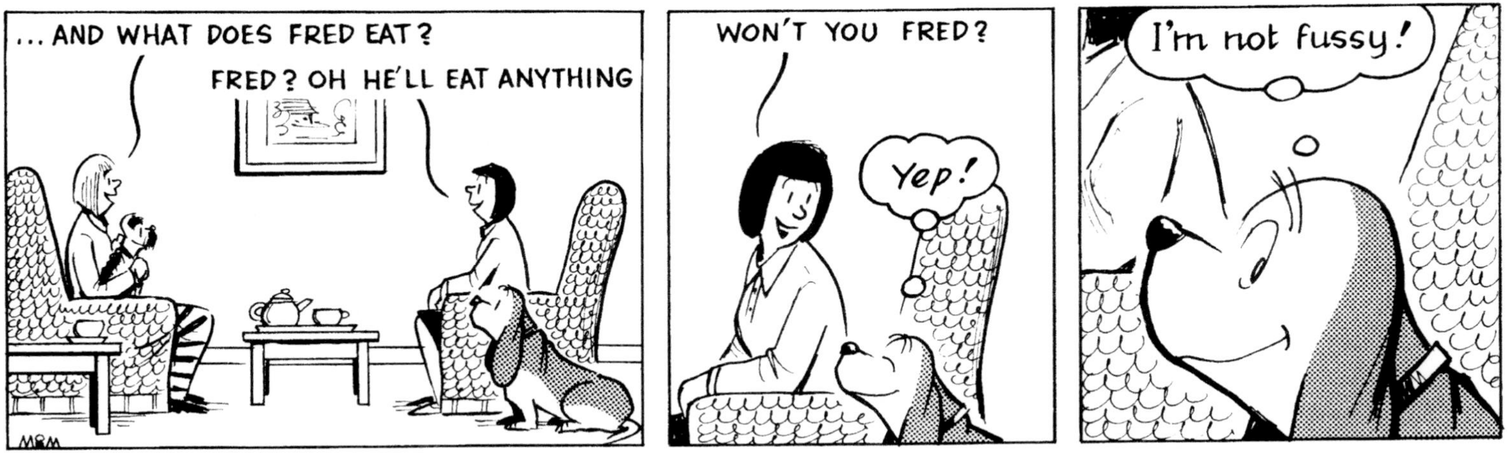
... AND WHAT DOES FRED EAT?
FRED? OH HE'LL EAT ANYTHING
MGM
WON'T YOU FRED?
Yep!
I'm not fussy!

2007

Here's a little challenge for you...
Spot the ball!
I THREW IT IN THIS GENERAL DIRECTION
WELL, IT MUST BE HERE SOMEWHERE

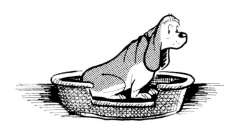

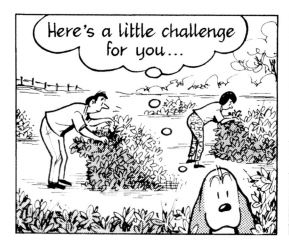

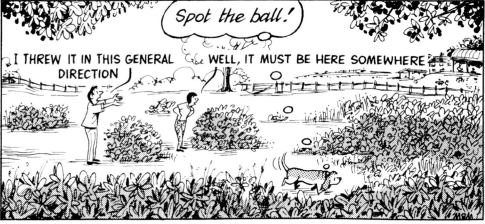

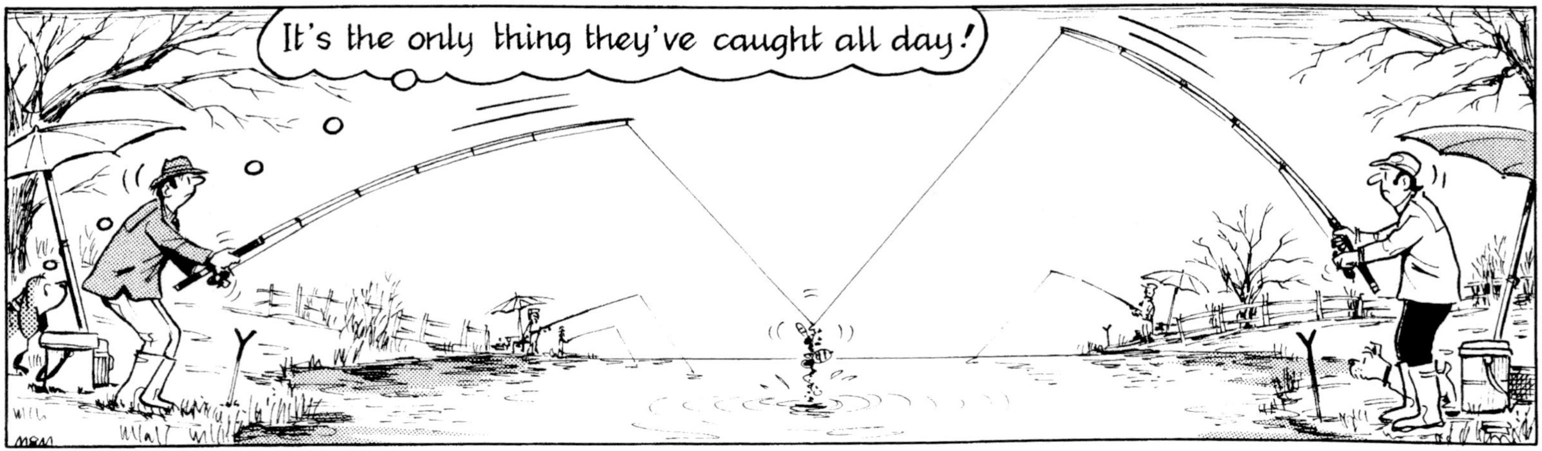
It's the only thing they've caught all day!

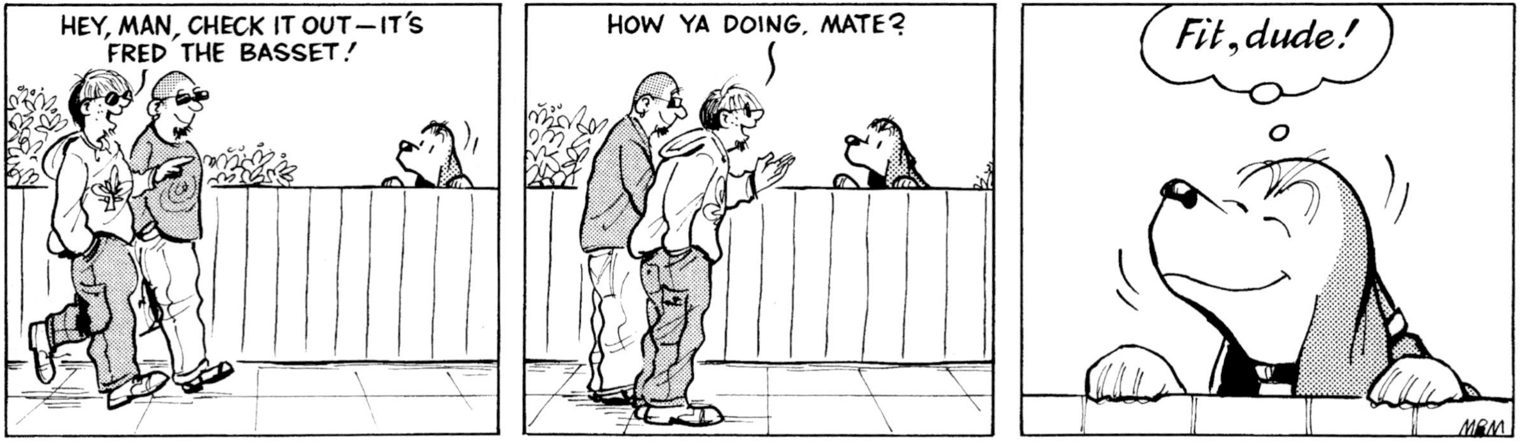
HEY, MAN, CHECK IT OUT—IT'S FRED THE BASSET!
HOW YA DOING, MATE?
Fit, dude!
MBM

2008

CAREFUL, DEAR!
No prizes for guessing what's going to happen next!
MARY-JANE
MARY-JANE

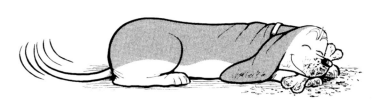

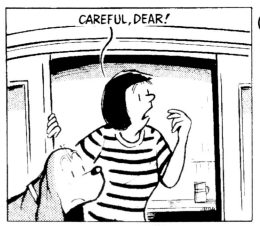

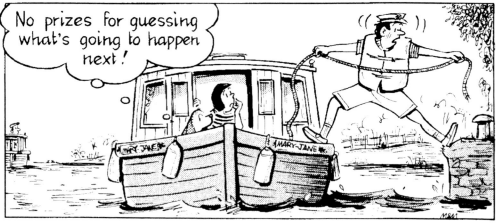

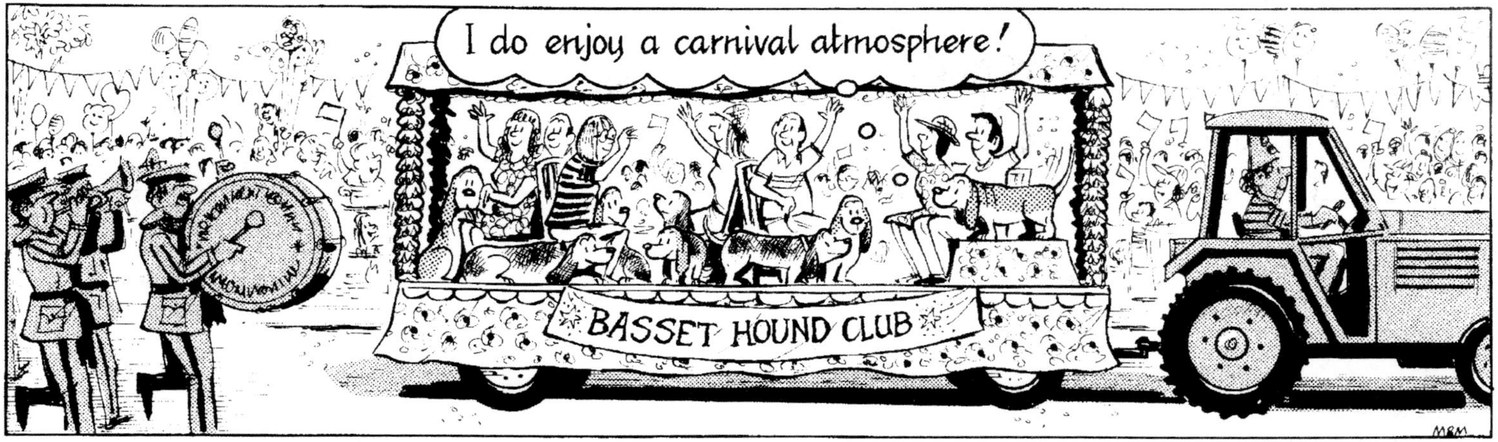
I do enjoy a carnival atmosphere!
BASSET HOUND CLUB
M&M

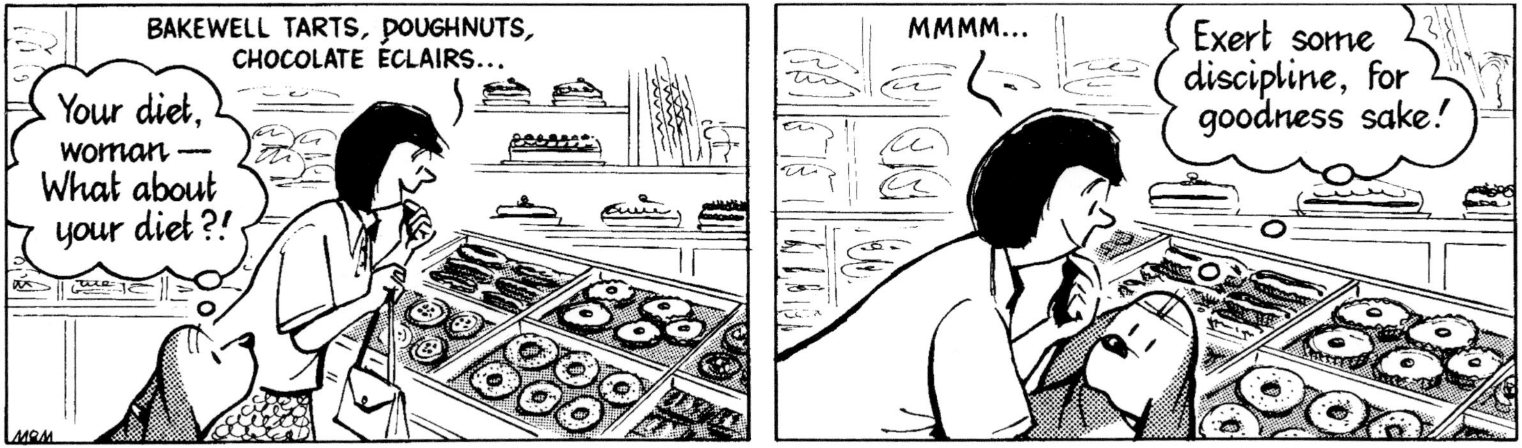
BAKEWELL TARTS, DOUGHNUTS, CHOCOLATE ÉCLAIRS...
Your diet, woman — What about your diet?!
MMMM...
Exert some discipline, for goodness sake!
M&M

2009

Life is so full of questions!

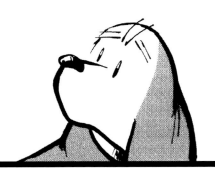

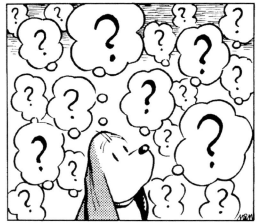

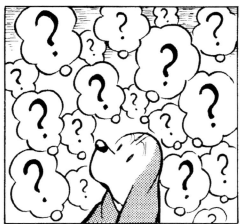

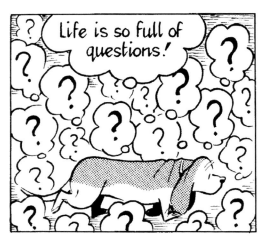

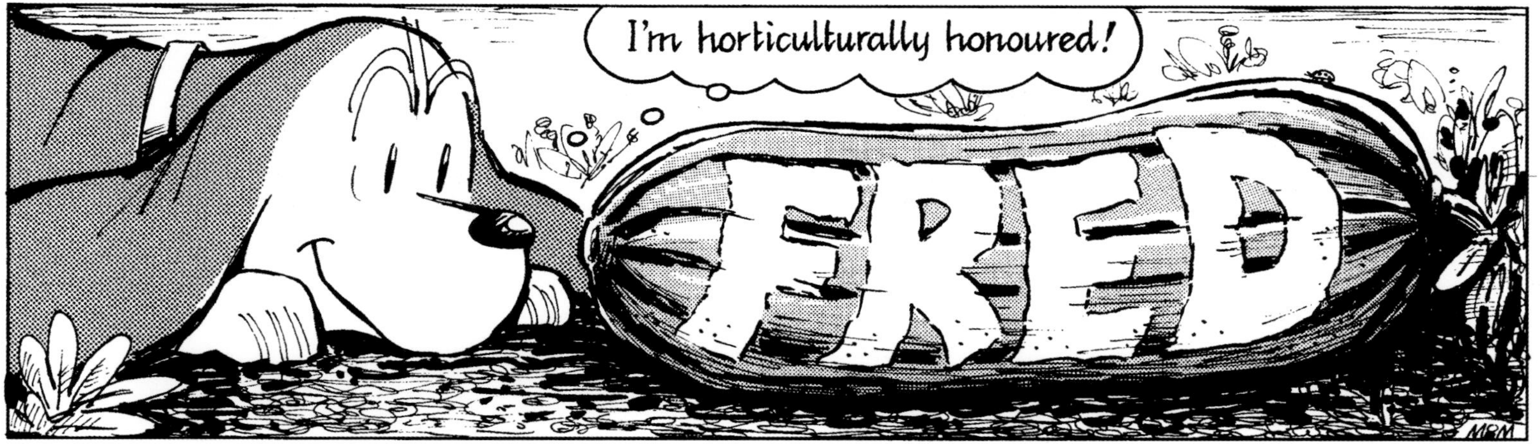
I'm horticulturally honoured!
FRED

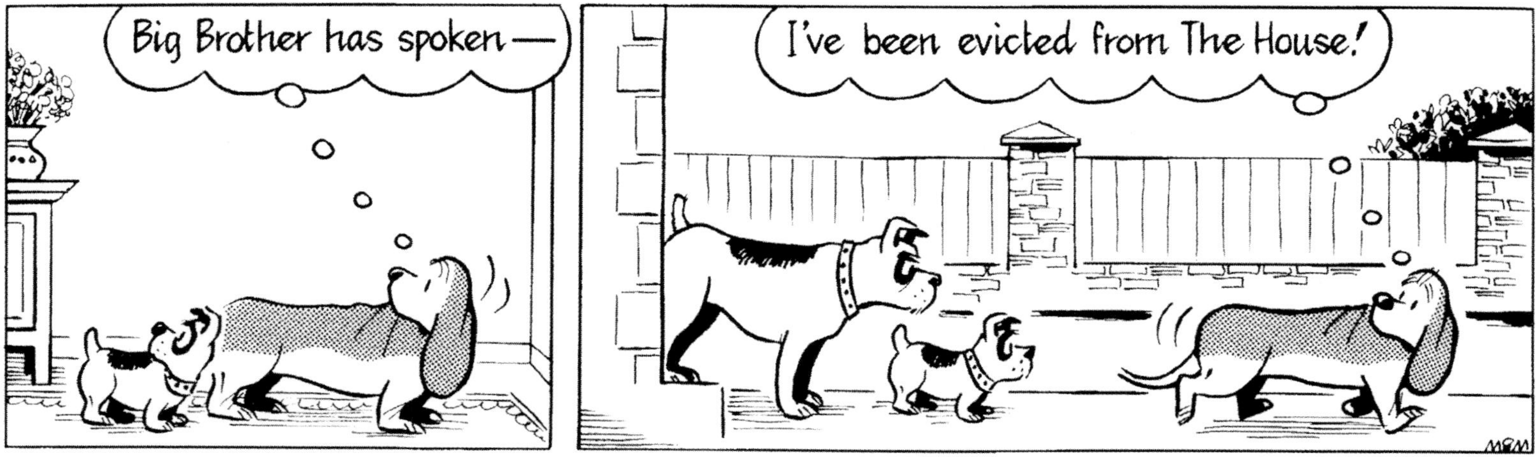
Big Brother has spoken —
I've been evicted from The House!

2010

Ooh, a new television!
Where's the rest of it, then?!

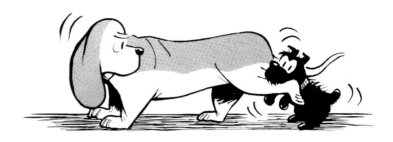

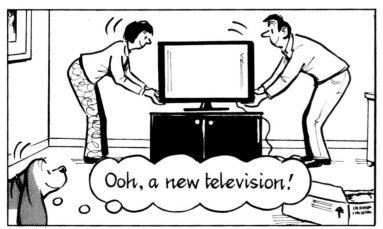

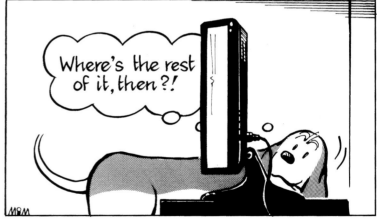

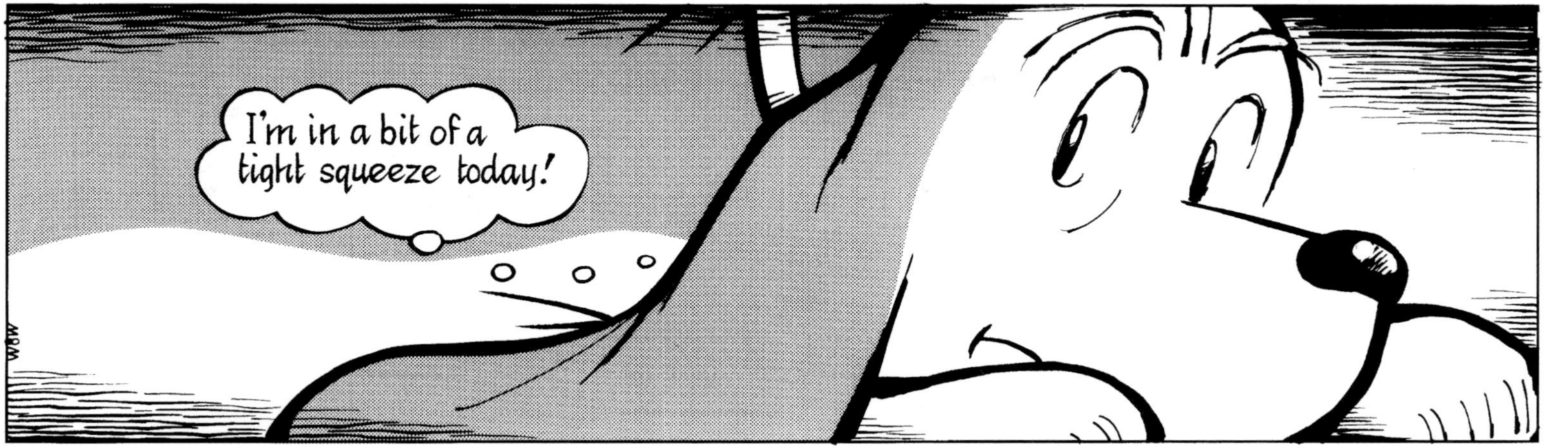
I'm in a bit of a tight squeeze today!

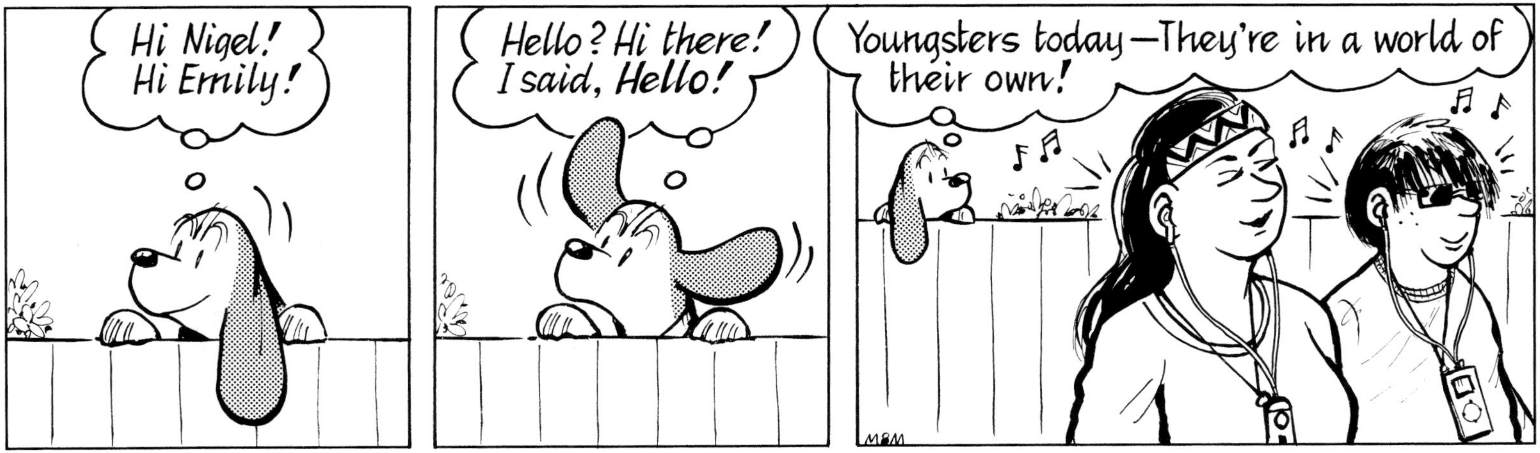
Hi Nigel! Hi Emily!
Hello? Hi there! I said, Hello!
Youngsters today—They're in a world of their own!

2011

He's busy this evening star-gazing—
Celebrity Gossip

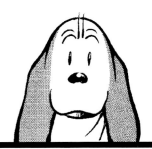

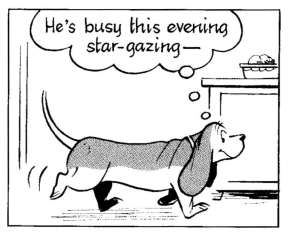

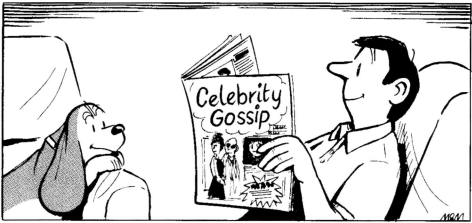

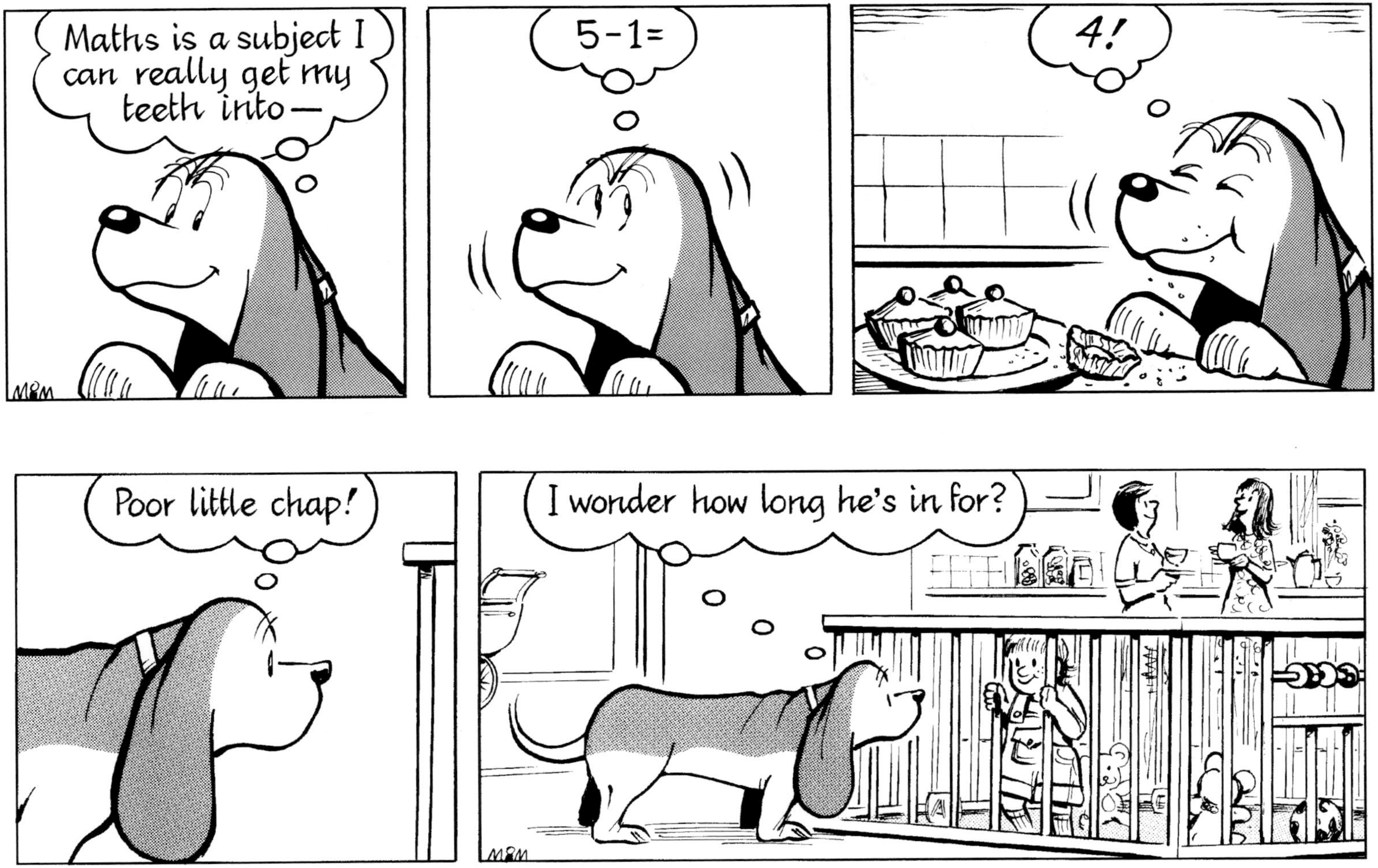
Maths is a subject I can really get my teeth into—
5-1=
4!
Poor little chap!
I wonder how long he's in for?

2012

CELEBRATING **50** YEARS

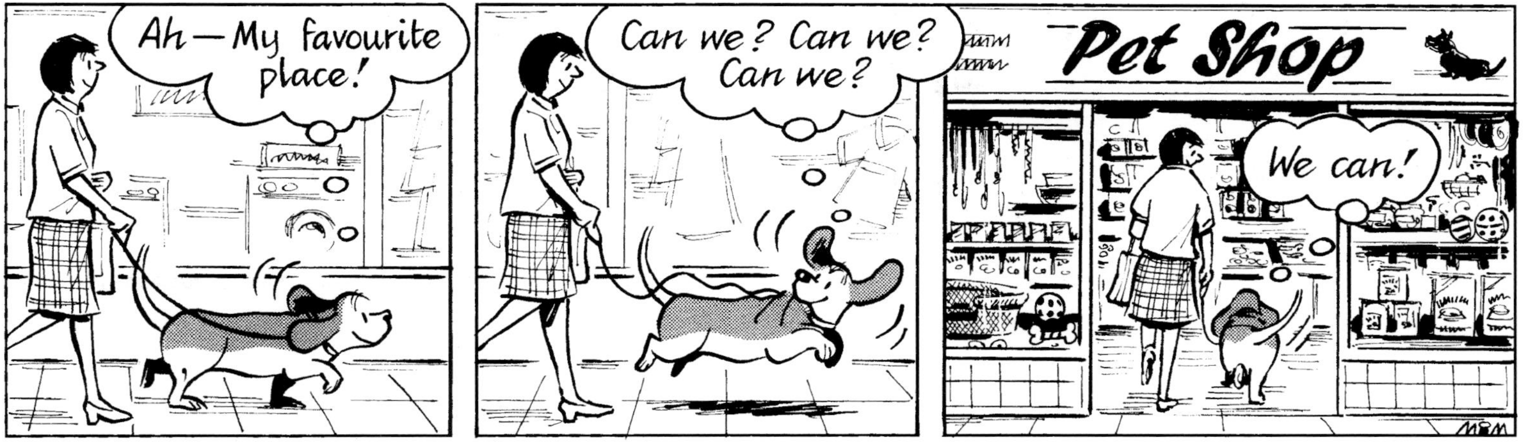
Ah — My favourite place!
Can we? Can we? Can we?
Pet Shop
We can!
MGM

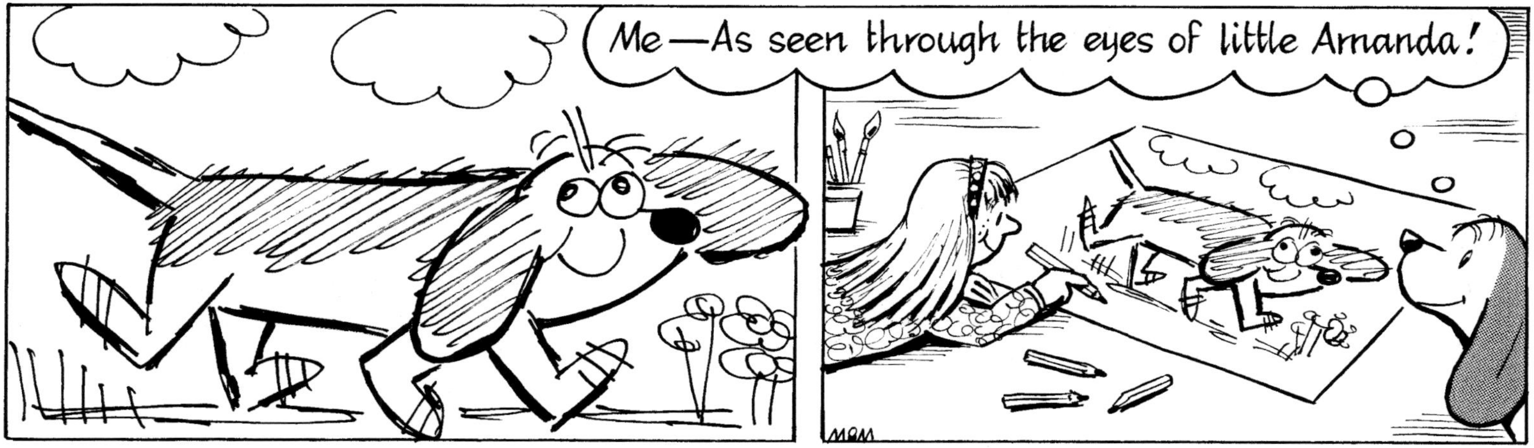
Me — As seen through the eyes of little Amanda!
MGM

2013

Ok, ok–I know they're not actually *my* sausages but it was *my* idea to steal them–
So–Two for you, three for me!
Deal or No Deal?!

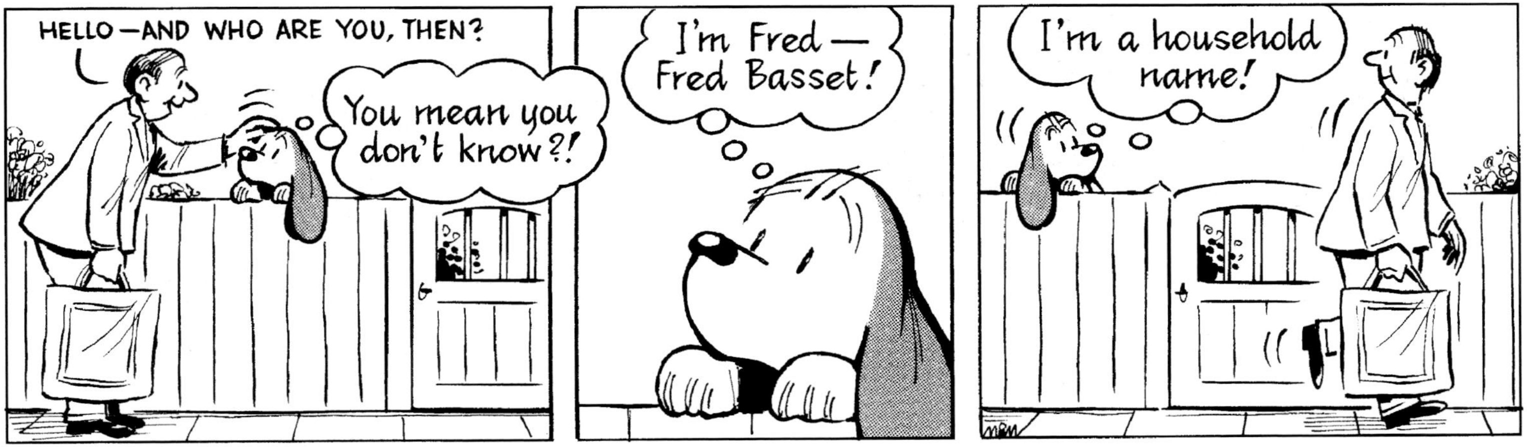
HELLO—AND WHO ARE YOU, THEN?
You mean you don't know?!
I'm Fred — Fred Basset!
I'm a household name!

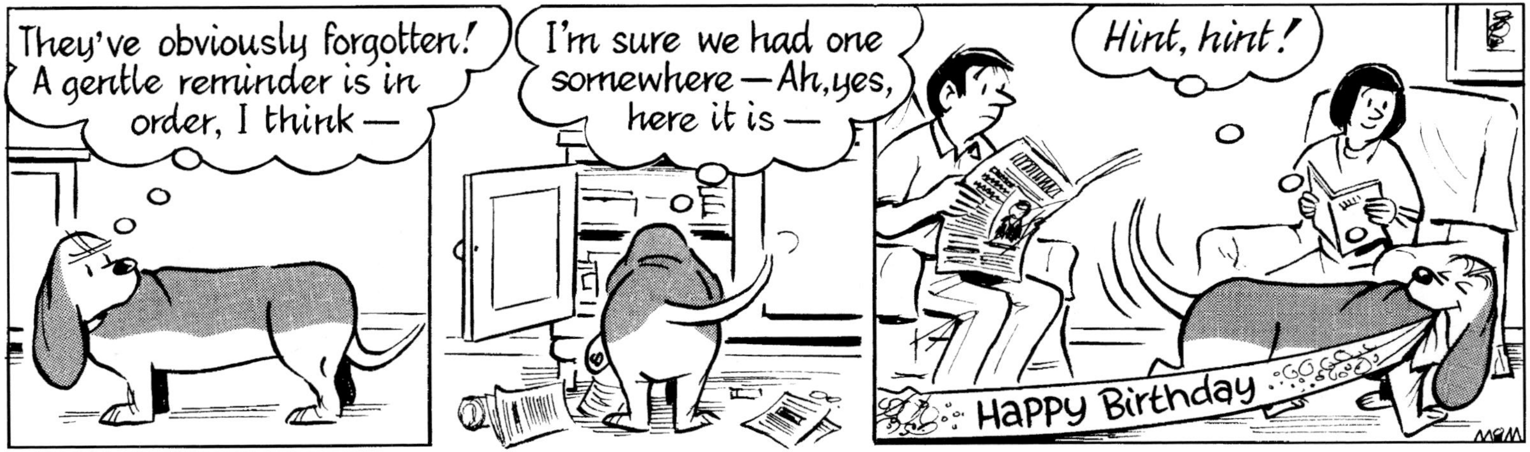
They've obviously forgotten! A gentle reminder is in order, I think —
I'm sure we had one somewhere — Ah, yes, here it is —
Hint, hint!
Happy Birthday

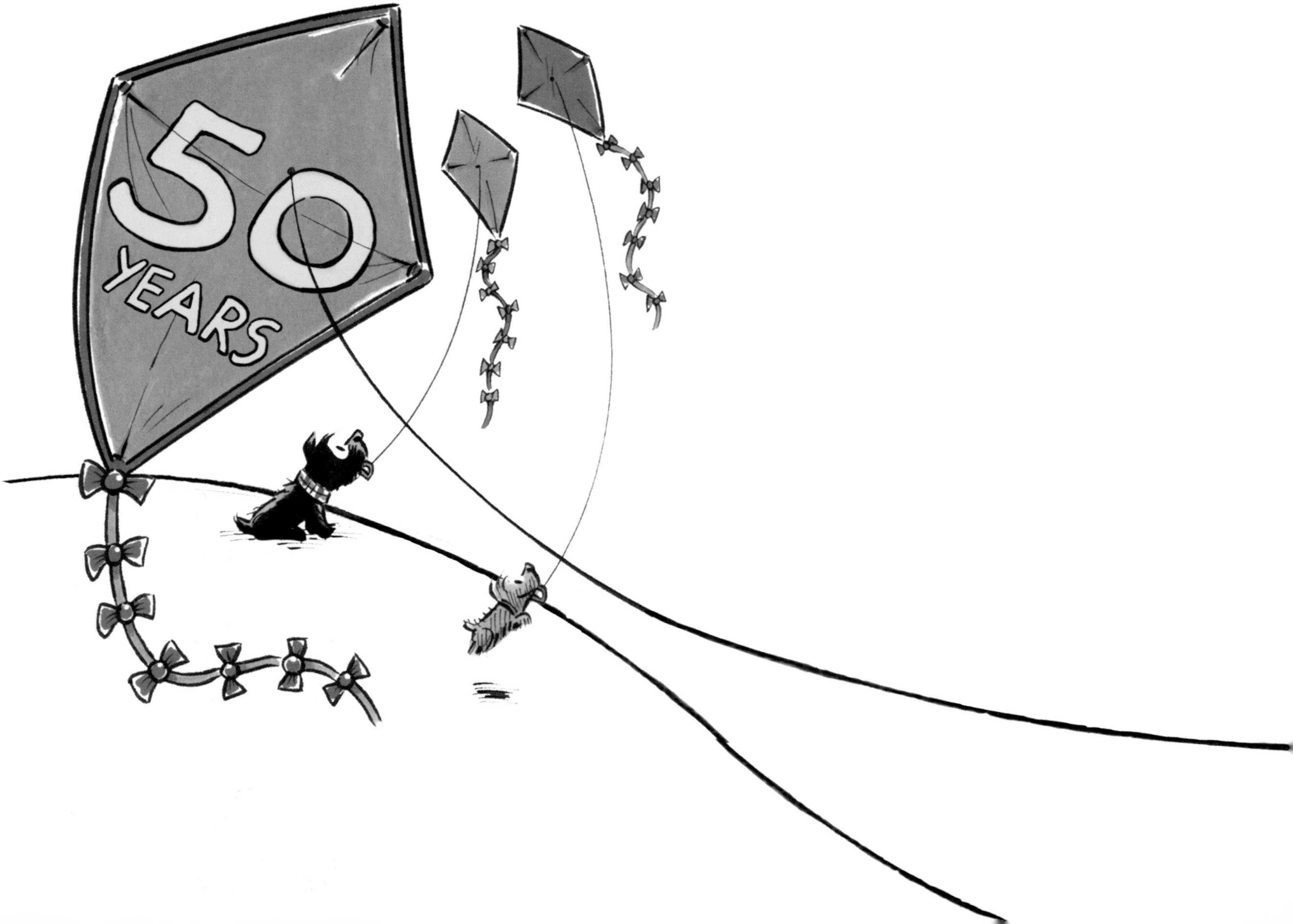
50
YEARS

Have you enjoyed this book?
If so, why not write a review on your favourite website?

If you're interested in finding out more about our books,
find us on Facebook at **Summersdale Publishers**
and follow us on Twitter at **@Summersdale**.

Thanks very much for buying this Summersdale book.

www.summersdale.com